Living on the Edge

Breaking Through Instead of Breaking Down

Elizabeth Wilde McCormick

ELEMENT

Shaftesbury, Dorset • Rockport, Massachusetts • Melbourne, Victoria

© Element Books Limited 1997
Text © Elizabeth Wilde McCormick 1997

First published in Great Britain in 1997 by
Element Books Limited
Shaftesbury, Dorset SP7 8BP

Published in the USA in 1997 by
Element Books, Inc.
PO Box 830, Rockport, MA 01966

Published in Australia in 1997 by
Element Books Limited
for Jacaranda Wiley Limited
33 Park Road, Milton, Brisbane 4064

Illustrations by Jeni Liddle
Cover design by Mark Slader
Design by Footnote Graphics
Typeset by Footnote Graphics, Warminster, Wiltshire
Printed and bound in Great Britain by
Creative Print & Design, Ebbw Vale, Wales

British Library Cataloguing in Publication
data available

Library of Congress Cataloging in Publication
data available

ISBN 1-85230-966-0

Contents

DEDICATION

This book is dedicated to Ian Gordon Brown 1925–1996,
with love and gratitude.

Acknowledgements

This book has emerged naturally from the giving of talks and experiential workshops on the subject of breakdown since my book *Breakdown* was first published in 1988. I owe a debt of gratitude to all those participants who dared to explore this difficult subject with me, at workshops in London, Dartington, Lowestoft and Edinburgh. I owe much gratitude to Barbara Somers for many things, but it was she who indicated to me whilst working together in Scotland that this book was *in potentia*.

I thank Ian Fenton who, in 1984, was my first publisher at Coventure, who commissioned the work for Element Books, and who gave generously of time and discussion on the early drafts.

My thanks to those who gave permission for their stories and images to be used to illustrate the ideas in the text. Acknowledgement is made to Faber and Faber Ltd for permission to use extracts from *Four Quartets* by T S Eliot, and *Collected Poems* by W H Auden, and to Element Books Ltd for the use of an extract from Dante's *The Divine Comedy*, translated by James Cotter. No person's material or images have been used without their permission.

Many people have helped me to consolidate my ideas for writing about the edge. In particular I offer deepest thanks to Belinda Ackerman, Shakir Ansari, Marjorie Orr, Renate Ogilvie, Annalee Curran, Nigel Wellings, Denis Payne, Simon Wilde, Ted Olive, Harriet Griffey, Mark Watson and Charlotte Du Cann, Geraldine Saabor, John McCormick, Barbara Somers and Ian Gordon Brown.

For research into anthropology and artists on the edge my thanks go to Kate Wilde for all her hard and creative work.

This book is the result of my own developing thoughts and whilst I am profoundly grateful to those above who helped me in the process, I take full responsibility for the ideas expressed in this book.

Introduction

Each one of us has a personal edge, possibly a series of edges throughout one lifetime. All of us can trace periods of time when we felt pushed to the edge of our personal capacity for coping. We wonder how we can go on; we wonder how we can bear it a minute longer. This may be related to life crises, to others' demands of us, our actual knowledge base, to our understanding, tolerance and feelings, or to a deeper struggle with the root metaphor for our life, which in turn relates to why we continue to live, and on what terms we should live. Most of us today are familiar with the edges between being and doing; between the 'me' who is seen by others and the outside world, and the private, perhaps hidden, 'me'. Many of us are becoming aware of the need for a spiritual awakening on both individual and collective levels. It is often our experience at the edge – however this edge may present itself, and there are myriad forms – that awakens us to the energy of a transpersonal (that which goes beyond) self and dimension. We may not be able to name it as such at the time and our experience may not be recognized by others. There are those among us who seek to find control systems for the emotional and irrational, and there are psychological and philosophical commentators who are naming the fact of collective spiritual emergency in which the individual voice is struggling to be heard. We may reach edges where it is we who draw the line, saying 'beyond this I will not go', and this may be to do with finding our individual or collective principles, or connecting with systems of morality or meaning.

We may feel at times that we need an edge in order to have something to go on because it is at the edge that we feel most intensely. Edges force decisions, what or who goes where. It is at the very edges of personal experience that a human being is most stretched and tested. At the edge we meet our demons and our gods. We meet our real selves.

Sometimes we are stretched creatively by having an edge. The structure of the edge, its deadline effect, brings out our very best. Sometimes we shrink from the edge and can only hover precipitously, feeling 'on hold', in limbo, paralysed by fear for what the edge might bring. Sometimes we plunge over the edge into our personal darkness.

Bearing the tension of the edge can also bear fruit, or call forth an awakening. The small beak of an infant chick gestated inside an egg breaks through the edge of shell to signal new life. Green shoots of spring press through the frosted earth edge of winter. These moments of realizing and transcending the edge are always compelling. They are both thrilling and potentially dangerous. They offer, as do all edges which lean into crises, danger and opportunity. Outside edges push us against the boundaries of ourselves and our everyday consciousness. To grow wise we must have an edge and we must meet many edges.

We may court the edge; we may become addicted to the edge; we may get pushed onto the edge by outside circumstances. Collectively we are, as the millennium approaches, inexorably linked to the edge of the 20th century. The compelling metaphors of our time are linked closely with the earth. Will it survive the impact of the human race upon it? It seems as if we have pushed its capacity to the edge of its limits. It now groans under the weight of overpopulation, and labours against global pollution and plunder. The progress myth of urban expansion and technological advance threatens and challenges the meaning and dignity of human expression. Any thinking person questions the nature of survival into the next century. What will be the values of the next millennium? On what terms will we live? Never before have the progress myths so dominant in the Western hemisphere been so challenged. We wonder whether we can go back and harness the ancient wisdoms of the past in order to find ways to live that do not threaten the actual fabric of the earth upon which we depend; or whether we have gone too far, become so dependent upon technological communications that our human muscles are grown slack. Or can we harness both developments in our life as human beings so that we come to the narrow path of the edge with wider deeper funds of knowledge, from both East and West, from both artist and scientist, from both masculine and feminine principles, but use it for a shared purpose.

Knowing what our personal edges are and what forces lead us there can be a way of becoming an edge-walker. We know then that there will be edges, and that they will teach us how to live even in the narrowest of places. Once we have recognized, walked, danced even, upon the many edges that invite us we forge within ourselves a strong centre that is able to live in every-day terms and at the same time make a connection with the dimensions of the soul. We do not become seduced by, held captive by, thrown over or collapsed into the edge any more than our journey demands. An opportunity to widen our understand-ing can emerge from our dance upon the edge, which cannot be realized in any other way. From the narrow place a breadth of strength and wisdom is forged. From the edge we get to know our extremes. The opposite forces within us have the opportu-nity both to keep their vital differences and to come together via the edge in a way that offers the true heartfelt energy of transformation. Then the edge becomes the place where we are invited to view most carefully the divisions that separate us, internally, externally and in our relationship with others and the world.

This book describes how the edge can be a place of soul forging. It outlines the properties and forces of the edge that make us dig deep inside, to find answers to life that the analytic capacities of our everyday personality structure cannot provide for us. By connecting to the transpersonal and soul dimensions, we become connected to all animate life, and are able to listen to the note of the soul and dance with its rhythm as it resonates throughout all the living and created world. In this way our world becomes a wider vision of all that we create both individually and as a collec-tive force, and we are not reduced, as psychology would often reduce us, to a limited world of inner pathology mirrored in out-side event.

The book offers a way to look at and work with our individual edges for the purpose of gaining the animate strength and wisdom needed for forging a soul, and the chance that this also brings for grace, laughter and happiness. The implicit thesis is that when we individually forge a strong centre and sense of soul this energy generates out to all that we do and are connected to in the world. We do not keep it for ourselves alone, but share the love that has come our way.

The understanding within this book comes from my work as a psychotherapist with a wide background in clinical work in social psychiatry, cognitive analytic therapy and humanistic and transpersonal psychology, and from my own experience as a human being on the edge. The main psychological and philosophical themes come from my involvement with transpersonal psychology for the last 22 years. The use of the image of the spiral comes from recent understanding that the spiral shape is at the core of our microscopic cell and plant structures; all life grows from this shape. And in the journey of a human life we tend to move in the way of the spiral, with life itself taking us back over the same place but from a different perspective. The view from transpersonal psychology is that in one life we make two journeys – the journey of the ego personality and the journey of the self – and that together the two create opportunities for soul. Knowing the difference between the two, knowing how to listen to the note of each and to respond to the demands of each, offers a way for us to learn to become edge-walkers and -dancers. People who have been there and have learned the language of this place individually have a unique contribution to offer in times of great change and dire need. We need edge-walkers to show us the way forward.

Living on the Edge seems to have emerged quite naturally as a progression from my interest in and studies of the heart and of breakdown that have been the subject of three of my earlier books, from 1984 onwards. In *Breakdown* I describe 'On the Edge' as the second phase of the breakdown curve. Since *Breakdown* was first published in 1988, I have seen more and more people who use this expression spontaneously and who are negotiating edges of many different elements. There is acute tension collectively. We all feel on edge, and there are many unknowns.

On a personal level, I have always been aware of living close to the edge and sometimes my life has rendered this edge pretty thin. Then in May 1992 I had the following dream: I was running along the cliff edge in Suffolk where I live, with the North Sea on my left, in a hurry. Something tapped at my right shoulder. I brushed it off impatiently, rushing on. It tapped again, and again I brushed it off. At the third tap however I turned round impatiently. A young man, dressed casually, with a patient, kind face was standing behind me. He was pushing a young woman who slumped pale and lifeless in a wheelchair. 'All we want,' he said, 'is permission to put up her easel.'

The dream still brings a surge to my heart. At the time, I knew that it was a vital dream, full of significance. I knew, in my head, that I had not given enough time to the 'artist' within. But the potency of the dream's intent was only fully revealed to me when I actually had to live body and soul, 'on the edge', reclaiming the energies of these two inner young masculine and feminine figures who had come calling. For in June 1992, one month after the dream, I was diagnosed as suffering from viral meningitis, encephalitis and labyrinthitis, which took me to – and beyond – the edge for the next two and a half years.

I honour this experience because it so beautifully illustrates Jung's understanding that we can 'know' something in the head, even write about it, but it is only when it touches us in the heart that we *truly* take note of it. I could make sense of my dream and work with the images, but when they really got hold of me, their intent was awe-inspiring, because it is so often just when we think we have sorted something out that we are challenged most. It reminds us that some much greater force is alive and well inside us which has something in mind for us and whose path we must be humbled to follow, especially when we have no idea where we might be going. It means that we must *never* reduce the power of the dream or waking image to rationality or intellectual presumption, but let *it* tell *us*. And how it does!

There is a difficult and omnipotent myth within psychotherapy and analysis that if you have worked hard on yourself and done enough therapy you are 'sorted', even 'whole'. And the fantasy is that this means never becoming unwell or getting out of balance. A few people were cross with me for becoming so seriously ill, one or two judged that I had not worked hard enough on my internal conflicts. But I was deeply fortunate in that my wonderful friends, family and colleagues, and also my clients and students, offered me the tenderest love and acceptance. It was as if they trusted me to go through this difficult process and come through. My gratitude for this beautiful gift is still fresh. I do not believe I could have emerged as robust as I feel without this love and non-judgemental guidance. I believe that this is wise midwifery and I refer to this theme throughout this book. Those closest to me stood alongside me and named the process of initiation, even when I could not see it; watched me struggle with myself before making suggestions, and held my hand in the darkest terrors when I was haunted by the thought of damage to my brain.

My view has always been that wholeness must include health and sickness, light and darkness, and the potential for good and evil. This book does not offer a solution but a journey of exploration of what purpose risking the edge truly serves. It pays the deepest homage to the self who has us and who invites us to forge soul.

Part One

MAPPING THE EDGE

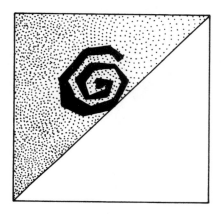

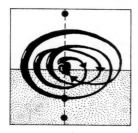

1

General Images and Definitions of the Edge

THE EDGE AS BOUNDARY

The edge is by definition a narrow place. It is limited and defined by the purpose it serves, to make a distinction between the hinterlands on either side. For an edge tends to come between two things. In this way it defines the boundary between one place or state and another. Even though narrow by definition, the edge may spread out to form a border, margin or verge, keeping the overall character of its purpose. Some boundaries are clear and robust, marked by potted plants, the songs of birds or army personnel with guns. Verges become the boundaries between two places such as a road and a house, and can be formed by grass-covered banks or painted lines. We also use 'verge' as an adjective as in 'verging on', meaning nearly or almost; we say 'verging on a nervous breakdown'. Or the edge can be formed by a brim or rim. When liquid reaches the limits of its container it is at the brim; it can also brim over, and we can brim over with affection or with fury, on the edge of sensing that our feelings are running over the brim or boundary, and into the next space: 'My cup runneth over.'

The margins of a page separate text from binding and give space for notes and anecdotes. People get shoved onto the margins of society when they are poor or homeless and become marginalized. And we speak of brinkmanship, taking a challenge to its utmost tension, the edge of surprise. Too tight a boundary and we keep too much out and what is inside suffers and festers for lack of change; too loose a boundary and all energy is scattered and the centre cannot hold.

THE EDGE AS SOMETHING SHARP

An edge in life can also be something as sharp as the thin blade of a sword, a knife edge or the cut of a blade. There are emotional edges to strong feeling, to anger, rage and violence, and the edges of despair and misery seem to offer a boundary of intensity beyond which our feelings sharpen or dissolve. We may pick up feelings of the edge or an edginess in the atmosphere when we are attuned to the drama of everyday life, on the streets of Lebanon or at a performance of *Macbeth*. These things pierce into us with their edge. Voices get an edge when under threat or siege. Edges of fear and terror press into us with cold steel. Feeling on edge can express itself in nervous excitement, irritation, the expectation of being about to burst with feeling or the sensation of being pregnant with change. We feel the edge of our fury, our own potential for thrusting with the sword of violence, and it is all we can do to keep our hand in our pocket. We may feel as if we are sitting atop a volcano about to erupt or caught in the swelling pod of a river that is about to burst its banks.

We speak of having an edge or urgency, seeing this as our slim advantage, the edge that we cling onto and cultivate. We may just edge our way cautiously when in new territory, or be at the cutting edge of science or creativity, that is, the place where the new is being forged amid the edge of effort, excitement and expectation.

NATURAL AND UNNATURAL EDGES

Some edges are natural, formed by the geography of outside, such as the edge that comes between two mountains to form a valley or pass. A beach or cliff offers a definition between land and sea. And these outside images are often taken inside symbolically, such as the image of walking in the Valley of the Shadow of Death, the cliffhanger in decision-making and games of dice or cards, even now in medical diagnoses. And cliffs, as at Beachy Head, can offer the literal places for the edges of life and death.

Each structure we create as humans produces an edge between the natural outside geography and the outside object that is created. We could say then that these edges are unnatural because they belong to the world of humans and are forced upon our natural habitat. Some structures such as harbours and houses may be built in sympathy with the land and seem to flow naturally out of it. We glory then in the meeting between human-made creative object and the natural poetry of the landscape. Others, such as electric pylons and high-rise hotels, can appear like unnatural intrusions, their alien edges blots on the landscape.

ORDINARY EDGES AS BOUNDARIES

The outside edges we know as part of our everyday life are shaped by the place where we live and the nature of our work. When we live in cramped rooms we feel the edges pressing in on us; or we may experience great beauty in the lines that delineate the edge of the flowing curtain against the wall and floor. A garden fence may provide an edge for roses or clematis, or a perch for robin and finch. Alternatively, the line that delineates our individual space from that of another may feel threatened, and we may have to fortify the edges of our space with barriers, locks and wire. In simple terms tables and chairs give form and edge to delineate where we sit and eat or make our bed. And, on an internal level, we all need to make boundaries between work and play, rest and activity. Sometimes the outside structures we create mirror the world we carry inside us. Perhaps there are times when we can only see ourselves as cramped and overcrowded inside, or when we feel homeless, as if we have no root; and at other times we are able to use more space, stretch out into new rooms and passages. When boundaries are not created we can feel overwhelmed or lost, looking for something to define us or give us shape.

Language has always carried a certain edge, which could keep us out if we could not speak the note, or which we could cross by learning new pronunciation or declension and following the language rules. Different, and difficult, languages are now more accessible and available for learning. The growing media coverage from different parts of the globe means that we are becoming aware of the vast range of language. At the same time we are collectively losing individual languages at a huge rate – over

2,000 languages have been lost from the Pacific Islands – as the need for common sign or communication grows. Some countries such as Wales and Ireland work hard to keep their language inheritance as their unique badge of identity. Language also no longer defines us as clearly as to our education, social class or economic group, which can be helpful, enabling, growing. But there are also losses, of style and music in language, often replaced by a bland monotonous character-free note, or a string of sloppy, jarring expletives.

MORAL EDGES

Whilst there are more edges in terms of matter in our culture – more objects to understand and look after, more decisions to make over how we should treat our bodies for example, accepting an organ transplant or foetal implant, taking powerful medications that alter mood and behaviour – there are fewer edges socially and morally. Very few types of behaviour are now considered morally reprehensible. Women who have babies and are not married are no longer considered morally defective as in the 1920s and placed in institutions or sent to the workhouse, nor are they forced into illegal abortion as in the 1950s. In fact the opposite occurs, and the number of children born to parents who are not married in the legal sense are growing, and thus the edge of the family, once a unit tightly controlled by church, law and society, is an ever-expanding changing unit of 'steps', 'fosters', and boy- and girlfriends.

Stories of personal tragedies, once a private matter for personal conscience and the balm of confession, are now sold shamelessly to newspapers for vast sums of money. The surge of litigation against professionals or personal friends to exact revenge or simply as a response to mistake, misunderstanding or once-accepted sad events seems epidemic. Professions are also specializing as a result, developing 'experts'. Soon therapists will also be divided into specialities and will be unable to give their common-sense opinion if they are not 'accredited' as to the speciality they comment upon. The reluctance or lack of courage to accept personal responsibility when appropriate has moved us as a society into the realm of magic control with no effort, where it is always someone else's fault. The state and the law then have to become the mighty arbiters, to try and solve what were once personal disputes, polarizing opinion and affecting the fortunes of many. We ask them to be the edge for us, relieving us of the very necessary limits that the edge provides. If there is no societal boundary on shameful behaviour we never face our own shame and work through its reality, so that we are released from its hold upon us. It is hard for common sense to survive when edges are relegated away from the personal. These edges of morality once held the boundary of acceptable behaviour; they gave us something to go on so that we knew where we were. Having the edge clearly defined, we could push against it or abandon it and take the consequences, or we could allow it to shape our personal life.

It is possible to 'sin' in the old-fashioned sense, and get away with it externally in society's terms. Stealing money, cheating on a business partner, drunk driving, murder and adultery no longer necessarily even lead to loss of friendship or transportation, let alone being beheaded! Countries where the boundaries of the law for crime are fierce but clear, such as having one's hand cut off, are penalized by more liberal countries, whose crime rate soars. Sin as defined by excommunication from a system of meaning and being confined to hell for eternity is less of a fear, except where Catholicism and Islam prevail as religious structures which hold the social system in their web. There seems to be less fear of moral judgement and punishment when there is no moral or religious code to offer a guide to the boundaries between right and wrong.

PEOPLE LIVING AT THE EDGE

People become marginalized when they cannot or do not find ways of fitting into social norms. At all edges of society and culture lie the shanty towns, encampments, temporary accommodation for people on the edge of the main social group. Tramps, 'bag ladies', vagabonds, beggars and squatters are part of all major cities and sophisticated cultures, as if forging a place for themselves when unable to fit in to the existing systems or culture.

Traditional travelling, Gypsy, tribal and nomadic people have always been linked closely with the earth and the natural world, as well as being seen to carry special psychic and prophetic gifts. They know the rhythms of the seasons and the movements of the stars and planets. They live simply. They may be carrying much of the soul and spirit of the world today. This is their only home. Often judged as 'antisocial' they in fact feel that 'to behave anti-socially is the proper expression for their marginal condition' (K Wilde).

For travelling people there is nothing more spiritual than the natural world itself; putting oneself above it would be pointless and dangerous. It provides everything needed for life. It is life.

There are few human groups which have not built structures. Until colonization by white Westerners the Aboriginal people lived all over the vast continent of Australia, building nothing and creating no pollution. Their cultural group is thought to have remained intact for 50,000 years. In their nomadic tradition they use a piece of land until it is in need of rest and replenishment, then they move on to let the land regenerate for other groups or for their return wanderings. Their edges and boundaries are interconnected like a honeycomb of spiritual, physical and cultural sharing: the needs of the group to eat, sleep and protect themselves from the elements, and to sing, dance and create ritual for change.

There are many who court the edge and are prepared to put themselves on the edge in order to bring back news of events in other countries. These are men and women who go over the borders to record the new and revolutionary edges of other countries and cultures, like war correspondents and photographers, whose home is a tent and mouthpiece their lens or letter. Then there are menders and healers, such as professionals working with Médicins sans Frontières. The explorers of mountains, ocean depths and ice caps put themselves on the edge of both the outside geography and their inside selves, sometimes 'touching the void' like Joe Simpson in the Andes. Firefighters, potholers – indeed all rescuers – work on the edge to meet others who have fallen from or lie clinging to it.

All people living in Western mental institutions and psychiatric hospitals are on the edge. We might say that they seem to exist in

8

the borderlands between what we have termed mental health and sickness, between 'madness' and 'sanity'. Their lives, for a time, are in the hands of professionals whose belief systems about their predicament will rule their treatment. The edges between madness and reason have throughout history been hotly debated. In *Psychiatry Inside Out: Selected Writings*, Franco Basaglia writes:

> Over the centuries, the rational and the irrational come to coexist, while remaining separate. Yet they are drawn closer once reason is in a position to neutralize madness by recognizing it as part of itself, as well as by defining a separate space for its existence. Such a process does not merely represent the evolution of science and knowledge. Nor does it signify the transition of madness from tragic experience in the world to sin, guilt, scandal, condemnation, and objectification of unreason – elements which, in our critical view are still fused and present in madness.

But clearly, anyone who exhibits wild, highly emotional or altered states, who sees visions, hears voices or dresses in a non-conformist mode, challenges the social, civilized order of the day. This, then, often becomes the boundary, and the voices go unheard, the visions unshared, the images uncharted. Those who have spent time in mental asylums and written about their experiences – such as John Perceval, the novelist Antonia White, William Styron, Anne Sexton – are all able to impart, with poetic clarity and reason, the stark images of their suffering whilst 'mad'.

THE ARTIST'S EDGE

Artists perhaps offer us a unique glimpse of the edge-walker and they often have periods in and out of 'madness' or delusion and depression. In common with travelling or nomadic people, artists need to be able to put themselves on edge in order to create the faithful image of their ideal. Turner once had himself roped to the mast of a ship in a full storm in order to capture the visual image of the light, the water, and its movement and feeling. In *The Artist's Eye*, Harriet Shorr writes:

9

The gesture of the brush is an expression of feeling aroused by the perception. Painting is not about objects themselves but about the process of seeing and painting them.

Artists often need to live in seclusion or as recluses, maintaining a position as outsider, and actually live on the edge of the group or society in order to be the observers, recorders, and commentators of the group and its history as a whole. Within the body of their work, each working day involves them pushing themselves against the boundaries of what has gone before in order to create the new: the cutting edge, concert pitch, vomiting in the wings, the agony and ectasy of creative tension, the threat of expulsion from outside at failure, the threat of inner expulsion when the creative act does not faithfully represent the inner sound or word. As Ann Egum notes, for Munch 'his dispassionate analysis of his innermost thoughts and fears demanded "an art which is the result of a compulsive need to open one's heart"'. It was a private symbolism wrought by his own traumatic experiences.

The Artist Within

We all have an inner artist who paints the inner life onto the canvas interface between inner and outer, thus creating everything in which we become fascinated and involved. Our dreams and fantasies, our hopes and fears, the way we play, those images and people and experience we are drawn towards are all initiated by the inner artist. The colours and shapes we choose, the sounds and dances to which we move, the tapestries we weave throughout our life, all originate via the inner artistry of each individual. When we look back and see the themes and threads of our life so far we can see the hand of the artist who has woven his or her way, always holding some thread or other, linking the different phases of our life. Even our symptoms, whether through body, mind or emotions, are created by the artist who uses whatever tools are available to make sure this language is kept alive. Symptoms are our main signalling device from our unconscious world. Much of this book will be drawing upon the inner artist to help us become edge-walkers.

10

THE EDGE AS DEFENCE

When we want to keep others out we build a wall inside us, or our body language shuts them out. We may need, and choose, to do this, and it may serve us well. But defences are never permanent. They may be built like external structures, with great effort and imagination, designed to withstand pressure and encroachment, and they may last for years until challenged by greater forces, like the sea defences in Suffolk and the great barbed and armoured wall dividing Berlin. It is as if defensive edges are built to be challenged and changed, however permanent they seemed. And behind the falling of each of the well-documented great structures is the huge, often unconscious collective pressure for change, whether from Nature's elements or from cultural pressure, so that when the edge is breached we must all change. And when we hold onto our internally built defences for too long we remain inaccessible, we lose the ability to communicate, our inner world becomes cut off, at risk of an autistic silence.

DYNAMIC AND RIGID EDGES

Edges keep things out and they also keep things in. When the edge becomes rigid it may not be able to let anything pass. It may just become a grotesque, redundant white elephant, only crumbling slowly with time like the stone walls and barricades that once formed the penal colony of Port Arthur in Tasmania, where children had cells and penal servitude for life was the norm. They remain as stubborn ruins to remind us of the stubborn structures we once created in an attempt to maintain one fixed view of human behaviour as laid down by law. And we fill our land with the products of waste – bottles, cans, nuclear fission – whose dead structures, with their lethal edges, no longer serve but threaten.

But when edges are dynamic they are open to change. Like an elastic band the edge may move with us at our own pace. As we change, so the edge changes. We bounce ideas, form thoughts, take on the edges of others, expand our awareness.

Even within the body itself, we can witness the rigid edges of 'disease' which has formed a structure which needs to be reduced by chemotherapy, cut out by scalpel, replaced by transplant or endured as an arthritic limb in a wheelchair, and also those structures which seem to have dynamic form and are therefore temporary. For example, the constrictions of the coronary arteries caused by the mind's response to stress are changed by rest. Palpitations and stomach cramps which can create the sharpness of spasm or the rigid outline of ulceration may be caused by a panic attack due to unprocessed feeling and might soften and heal in response to a listening ear rather than action upon the structure. Sometimes the edges need both responses.

EDGES OF CONSCIOUSNESS

Less clearly defined edges are those inside us, our internal edges, such as those between consciousness and unconsciousness, between altered states, dream and trance states, memory recall, those aspects that are in the light and those in the dark. There are some edges between body and mind, or between our functions of thinking, feeling, intuiting and sensing. They are harder to delineate, and often become blurred and confused. In order to live fully we need an overall balance of body–mind interactions, knowing which are which, as well as the interweaving of each of the functions.

Then within the whole personality there are edges between one sub-personality and the next. Part of us may feel small and helpless, like a child, whilst part is fierce and 'grown-up'. One part may grow larger than another, its edges spilling over or blocking another's path. These are dynamic edges, edges which can be noted and named, whose shape and edges are for changing. Some parts of us need the appropriate boundary to form an appropriate edge, as we filter information, deal with crises, take on as much as we are able. Systems are blown when the edges become overloaded, as in some experiences of rage or grief. Or when the unconscious life of a person fills all available space, the boundaries holding the personality together break down and the centre cannot hold, as in some forms of breakdown.

Problems seem to occur when edges between one inner state

of being, or sub-personality, are too defined and have become separated from awareness of the living whole, as in a person suffering multiple personality structure. Or, conversely, edges between consciousness and unconsciousness which are too poorly defined can result in psychosis and schizophrenia. One person described their image of being on the edge as being on the high wire and jumping from one trapeze to another with the moments of suspension between the two. Other people have talked about being cut adrift when familiar ground shifts and the moment holds nothing known.

For all thinking people, the divisions between knowing and not knowing, between feeling and not feeling, between what constitutes madness and sanity, are all open to question and opinion. But we long for an edge to define them for us, to give us clear guidelines, a clear path to follow, to gain us some control.

INDIVIDUAL DEVELOPMENT

We are born into families that represent the soil into which our individual seed of selfhood is planted. Very few seeds find the environmental soil just right for their natural development. There is always some adjusting to do, a necessary adaptation to the family into which we find ourselves born. Some seeds are 'bonsaied', even thrown onto stony ground. Some of us have to develop quite rigid adaptations to the life we are born into and these are important, for they serve us well. The shell into which we crawl in order to exist in the outside world keeps us safe – for a while. But at some point the seed of our nature will rebel at the enforced entrapment. We then come up against our own inner edges, the edges between who we have had to be in order to survive and who we really are, and the process of reframing those edges becomes paramount.

THE EDGE AS THRESHOLD OR LINK

The edge is also a threshold in the way that the beach is the threshold from sea to land and land to sea. A gate or door, a porch or vestibule, offers a place of threshold. When we step over the threshold we pass from outside to inside and vice versa, from one place or state to another. Some thresholds are wide and spacious, like the great marble vestibules or decorated anterooms of 18th-century stately homes. Some thresholds are watched over, by guards or servants, by janitors or jailors. The keeper of the threshold can be a figure like Janus, the Roman god of the portal, whose two faces look both in and out.

Thresholds may have a very thin edge and feel flimsy, like the flap of a Bedouin tent or the small entrance to a rabbit burrow, and may be without lock or key, fanfare or watcher. But the purpose is the same: to create a distinction between one place and another, and to name formally the process of passage, the threshold itself. We talk about being 'in transit' when in between countries; we are 'in passage' whilst moving through the in-between phases of life; we are 'in transition' as we experience change. We move into the anteroom before entering the room of our destination; we enter the 'post' period after an experience or place, as in post-natal depression or post-traumatic distress disorder. Falling 'over' or 'off' the edge quite suddenly when we are not looking, or when we are doing something else, speaks to our experience of the edge in an internal sense, when we are plunged from one state of being into another. The threshold then is absent, or hidden perhaps within events which preceded it, and it can only be seen clearly with hindsight. Many people who are thrust into a spiritual experience or a *kundalini* awakening feel their bodies taken over by a powerful physical sensation. Others speak of falling in love, being caught by a psychological complex or archetype, being taken over by the forces of fate where the swiftness of the experience is a vital ingredient in the process. The inference is that without this lack of threshold we have no choice to turn back; we are pushed onwards into the journey the self has chosen for us, with neither time nor hesitation to hinder us.

And there are those other passages where the threshold seems to be endless grey monotony and we are kept waiting, seemingly in limbo, in suspense, with life on hold. Other thresholds come ready with all the uniformed attendants, some perhaps in white coats bearing syringes and electric shock treatment. Others still may be via the passages of war, being sent to another country or away to school or university, through a relationship or religious experience, or they may be crossed by death.

The threshold has been well marked in literature and art, as in the sentimental carrying of a bride over the threshold of their shared home by her husband, symbolizing his ownership and strength and her passivity. Jacob's ladder reaches up to heaven from the ground with its myriad steps. It is both the threshold and the journey itself, but also a link between the earth and the Divine. For Dante the gates of hell, immortalized by his poetry and the paintings of William Blake, were signposted 'Lay down all hope you that go in by me'. Once through, accompanied by Virgil 'with a face so joyous it comforted my quailing', he began one of the richest and most moving journeys recorded.

Thresholds in the inner developmental sense, such as that between girlhood and womanhood or boyhood and manhood, the biggest change we as humans make biologically, are marked by the passage of puberty and adolescence. For many cultures this has been marked as a threshold by rites of passage rituals and initiation ceremonies, with dancing, fire, chanting, special clothes and rites such as the shaving of a warrior son's head by a Masai mother. It may be religious structures which hold and carry out these passages, or edges, offering Barmitzvah or Confirmation.

WALKING THE THIN LINE BETWEEN OPPOSITES

The edge may be created by the tension between polarities, between the opposites of dark and light for example, of day and night, good and evil, masculine and feminine, sun and moon. The extreme tension of the edge may be challenging us to meet the opposites we hold inside or outside and find a third position or transcendent function for the extremes. For when two energies are polarized, nothing can happen and no life can flow. Some of us emerge into adulthood believing we can only be either X or Y. We are either perfectly in control or making a terrible mess. Whilst we may have survived by our rituals of control, over time the lack of balance will begin to bother us. Our control rituals may become more severe as we begin to fear them slipping. Or

15

life may plunge us into a 'mess' where we have to get our hands dirty and face all the fear this entails. We then journey at the edge until we find a third position which is not either/or, but which moves us into a closer homeostasis with the qualities held polarized as extremes.

THE VALUE OF THE EDGE AS THE PLACE OF CHANGE

At the edge we are caught in the liminal space, the moment in between, between where we have come from and something beyond, something new or alien. We are in an unclassified place. The edge carries the tension between what has gone before or where we have come from and what is to be. There are often no safe places, no boundaries, no classifications to help us define what is happening. We are thrown onto the suspense of the unknown and at the mercy of the lens through which we view our life as a whole.

It is a huge challenge to decide how we view and use any edge and what is on either side of it. For it is our view of either side that creates the edge in the first place. Attitudes to the structure and content of right and wrong, there and not there, being and doing, fair and unfair, nice and nasty, happy and unhappy, what we feel we can do and not do, form the nature and geography of the liminality of the edge. Being able to feel into its properties, its potential character based upon where we find ourselves in time and space, and becoming the explorer who looks both at where we have come from and to an image of where we might be going, will allow us to be in this place. Just these ideas can help us to weather this difficult place and move on to become the most creative of travellers.

Our journey throughout this book is to explore the very nature of the edge we find ourselves on and any future edges we may encounter. Our images of the place may change, as will our range of feeling. The emphasis is upon creative map-making, even when our only guide is the idea of a slim thread or a distant light or lamp in a dark landscape which someone else may be holding for us, and even when we cannot actually see the thread or light. However narrow the line, dim the light or alien this place, it is of ultimate value that we pause enough to give ourselves time to view things properly, even to bring in fresh lenses. Then the edge becomes the forging place, the place where new inner dimensions are created. Often what seems new and lessens the narrow tension of the edge involves simply accepting the old in a new way. Some people teeter about on the edge for fear of going over it into something worse than what has taken place before. Some freeze upon the edge. Others plunge over it in desperation.

Every passage in life involves a journey. Our method of transport may include going by bus or train, the collective forms of transport; or we may go it alone, rowing a boat, driving a car or motorbike, using roller skates or skis, or simply on foot. Most long journeys involve preparation, and we will be looking at what sort of rough guides or maps we might use in unknown territory. There will be times when we need shelter or a place to rest. There may be times when we have to ford a stream or find or create a bridge for the deeper waters. Birds and animals may join us, other friendly travellers may accompany us. The journey on the edge is no different from geographical journeys except that our method of transport and the way of our travel is held within our imaginations. Images of the style and atmosphere of our journey, of the safe places and horizon ahead offer the potential for helpful companionship. Alone the edge can seem a grim and hostile place, our dreams and inner life prey to murderous forces and evil giants, or we may face the terror of believing ourselves to be on the edge of annihilation, lost, abandoned, in the void, alone for ever, doomed to travel like Pilgrim, or Adam and Eve expelled from the green Paradise Garden, to walk in dirt, dust and excrement, to crawl naked and wide-eyed, unable to sleep like Nebuchadnezzar.

And this is frequently how we can cope with the edge: by witnessing and bearing the grimness and hostility, we change the edge from a fearful place we are likely to fall off to a place of initiation or rite of passage. Then we move from one attitude to another, one level of self-understanding to another. And when our feet and hands have become accustomed to the climate and landscape of the edge we are never quite so afraid or avoiding.

17

From this place we walk on to see what has actually been awakened, what is dawning ahead of us as the edge merges into the creative threshold. However long it takes, whatever the nature of the struggle, we find we have wakened to a wider dimension and have forged a bridge between known and unknown, and we may hold the place familiar for others.

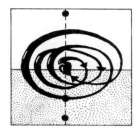

2

Naming Our Individual Edges

Many of us use the expressions 'I'm all on edge' and 'I'm living on the edge'. They may describe a feeling that lasts for a short time – a day or week – or it may hover for months and years, even a whole lifetime. The feeling will vary in intensity, but alongside it will be a longing to be relieved of it, to find a solution and get off the edge as soon as possible. For humans find it very difficult to live in a crowded, restricted way and in a state of constant emergency. We may recognize feeling on the edge and try and understand it by relating it to actual situations, something going wrong at work or at home, for example, something to do with a current relationship, or a decision that must be made. We may believe our edginess is related to our not being able to get over a particular loss or relationship, or perhaps we have been feeling physically unwell. We may have tried many solutions to bring about change. Being given a reason for the feeling, a diagnosis and suggestions for a concrete solution, or having an illness labelled, for which there may be treatment, can bring temporary relief. The 'mid-life crisis' is often used as an overall metaphor for the edge, but although we may have a name for it, and a rough understanding of what it is, we still need to map and reach into the alien territory. However, whatever its origin, if the feeling of being on the edge persists, or if it comes back after external changes have been made, then the answer that the edge is calling forth from us is most likely to lie within ourselves and our attitude to our life.

This chapter offers some ideas that might help us to gain insight into our own suffering and thus begin a new relationship with ourselves. We need to have some form of guide or map to help us to find out where we might be in relation to our life so far, where we have come from and what we might be seeking in the future. Living on the edge usually means that we feel stuck or suspended, often as if all that has happened to us has become in some way irrelevant, or holds no value at the present time. In *The Divine Comedy*, Dante writes:

> Midway this way of life we're bound upon,
> I woke to find myself in a dark wood,
> Where the right road was wholly lost and gone.

IDENTIFYING WHEN WE ARE ON THE EDGE

The following sections show the kind of sensations that help us identify when we are on the edge.

Feelings

These are the feelings that may indicate we are on the edge:

- feeling trapped or cornered; images of being in a cage
- feeling as if walking on eggshells; images of fragility, small creatures
- feeling a need to hold onto something lest we fall; images of falling
- feeling as if there are no choices; images of false imprisonment
- feeling alienated, marginalized, alone; images of being left on the moon
- feeling desperate, despairing, wanting a way out, feeling suicidal; images of death
- feeling as if 'nerves are all on edge'; images of being skinned
- feeling 'in limbo' or as if suffering a 'terrible waiting'; images of being sentenced
- feeling constantly afraid, or in dread, as if something terrible were about to happen; fearful images of impending doom
- feeling constantly angry, either bottling up rage or blurting it out inappropriately as in a tantrum or flinging fury at others who do not really deserve it; images of fire, fighting, war, guns, volcano

20

Body

The following bodily sensations may also be apparent:

- physical tension carried by the neck, shoulders and back, chest, arms; images of being in a vice, crab claws digging in
- disturbances in breathing, such as breathlessness, holding breath, hyperventilation, not getting enough breath; images of lack of air, longing to be high up in the air
- possible persistent headaches, nausea; images of hammers in the head, a lead ball in the stomach
- fatigue, exhaustion; treadmill images, man in a box, running for a moving train
- sleeping poorly, waking frequently or sleeping heavily, waking unrefreshed
- appetite changes, overcontrol of food such as feeling obsessed about eating, not eating by forgetting to eat or avoiding eating
- minor physical difficulties such as poor digestion, constipation, menstruation problems, sprains, twists, back pain, stomach irritation
- accidents ranging from scraping the car and twisting an ankle to collision and fracture

Mind

Being on the edge can lead to:

- confusion of thoughts, inability to think clearly, and accelerated thinking
- obsessional ideas and thinking (ruminating compulsively on one word or idea); obsessional thinking can be seen as the result of unmanageable feelings taken up into the thinking function, in order to try and sort them out, but creating an *idée fixe*.

Paranoia is a medical term used to describe a state of unreality. The word derivation is from *paranoesis* which means literally 'mind always preoccupied'. When the edges feel rigid, as in some states of paranoia, we fall into the grip of believing our paranoid

21

thoughts or fantasies literally. When the rigid edges are challenged to become more dynamic we are able to hear our voices with a poetic ear and not take them or act upon them literally. Then we are able to take relief from the incessant edge of demand that paranoid moments inflict upon us.

Loss of Connection with Intuition and Spirit

Being on the edge often feels as if intuition and spirit are eclipsed. They can be hard to reach when all our energy is taken up with surviving the narrow ledge. It is as if we just cannot let go, or take any risks. Once we recognize that we are in the place of the edge, connecting again with our own inner wise observer can help us to locate our spiritual self and to regain or to develop the powers of our intuition.

We can begin to recognize that intuition and spirit are in eclipse by asking ourselves when we last felt joy, experienced real pleasure, or were drawn into the soul of music, poetry and dance for its own heart's sake. In Part Two we will be exploring how contacting our own wise guide or observer can take us through the journey we must make, from dangers of the edge to the edge as a threshold for the next part of our journey. It is in making the movement in attitude, from clinging on to what is habit because of a fear of falling to choosing to jump, that we gain control over what feels as if it has control over us.

Feeling out of Control

When body, mind and feelings become out of balance, with one function overloaded, and we feel out of touch with intuition and our spirit, we begin to feel as if the whole of us is out of control. It is useful to ponder on the fact that all spiritual paths begin with an experience of going out of control. At first when we feel like this, we tend to cling on to what is familiar, however old and worn that habit may be. If we have to cling on for a long time our energy diminishes and we lose contact with anything meaningful. People speak of feeling 'cut off' from anything of beauty or meaning. It is as if we can only be captives of our old ways, only able to peek at life outside through a tiny crack in the fence or wall that limits us. Some describe their experience of the edge as like being captive on a vast ship bobbing about on swirling sea, or in a car whose brakes have gone, or imprisoned in a cage or fortress where the only evidence of normal life going on outside is muffled sounds through walls. When we feel trapped and out of control we may long for freedom, to link with something that makes us feel at home to ourselves. That special note held in beauty and poetry, song, dance, fun, pleasure, the inner music of our soul is far away, even absent, and seems to elude us.

On the edge we feel unable to relax, use humour, let go into any form of pleasure. It is as if some great censorious hand holds us back. We may find ourselves postponing: 'I'll wait until . . .' As we fear losing control, we tend to try and reassert that control in the ways most familiar to us, the ways that we have previously used. We may seek it by not allowing any feelings, for example, so that we shut down all close contact with others. We may try to think our way out of things, making more and more lists, demanding more and more letters or memos, making unnecessary phone calls, trying to 'read' or 'think' our way out of a fear of the unknown. We may try and work harder physically, if that is what we know, believing that once a certain goal is achieved we will feel better. But the opposite tends to happen. We feel as if we are running faster and faster, but our world is getting narrower and narrower, and as our anxiety and levels of stress rise so our actual functioning and performance drops. We may feel like Sisyphus, forever doomed to push a boulder up a hill.

Many of us in this place try to use willpower alone to keep going. There is the fantasy that if only we can assert ourselves in the right way, go on for long enough, everything will fall into place. We may find ourselves secretly relying on magic to bale us out, we may be drawn to fortune-tellers or psychics who offer an instant cure. We may find solace in alcohol, drugs, sex, new and risky relationships, or driving very fast. We become prey to images that offer a way out of our dilemma - jumping off a bridge, disappearing, changing identity. We unconsciously begin to court the crisis of the edge to bring about resolution. The force of using constant willpower pushes us into a left-brain attitude, eclipsing the right hemisphere which is responsible for our ability to relax, play, recuperate and make appropriate judgement. So the methods we may feel compelled to try when we rely on willpower alone do not serve us. In fact they exacerbate our situation, and may precipitate a crisis. And often, this is all we can do because it is all we know how to do. Even those of us who 'know' that this is the wrong way to do things find ourselves spinning and running at certain times.

Having identified that you have many of the feelings associated with being on the edge, there are several ways of placing the questions 'why?', 'why now?' and 'what does this mean for me?' into context. Our journey along and through the edge can be helped by having some idea about what purpose our being there serves.

IMAGES OF THE EDGE

All of us have visual images. If we are asked to imagine a green field in summer, we can see it in our mind's eye. We may also be able to feel the warmth of the sun on our skin, smell the clover or honeysuckle in the warm summer air, see a bird or a butterfly resting on a buttercup. We can also probably feel the atmosphere of the green field and be able to look into the quality of the grass, its length, strength, lushness. There may also be other images that come to us in this field of their own accord, without being suggested, like water for example, or a mountain, or sheep and cows.

Before we developed words, the world of the image was prime in all our lives. The touch, smell, feel, sound of our interuterine and nursery years are all recorded within us as images. The touch of a hand, for example, is an image. It may be amplified to become the soft embrace, a firm holding or a fierce slap. The hand will be the hand of a person who has meant something to us. We may also carry this image and seek to find it metaphorically, such as wishing to be held in a cradle of care during times of loss and bewilderment, or the longing to be held by the embrace of the Divine. Images remain unconscious until triggered by something happening in our conscious life. A conversation with an old friend about schooldays may bring into consciousness an image of the schoolroom, the voice of a teacher, the smell of school dinner or the memory contracted into the stomach wall of taking examinations.

Images may appear to us in dreams, and come charged with feelings and animation that do not allow us to forget or discard them. Being on the edge, brings it own vital imagery: of the cliff edge, the well, the waterfall, the bridge, the mountain pass, the chasm, the dark pit, the cage, walking a tightrope, falling from a parachute, at sea with only a tiny liferaft, suspended above the high trapeze. Variations of these images have been shared with me by people who have identified feeling on the edge, and who felt that the visual image connected them in feeling and meaning with that place.

Images serve us well because they come from the place within our imagination that is not contaminated by will. Images are universal language. The ego–will *may* take up an image for its own purpose, but the origin of the image is that rich world of imagery that unites us, moving us from our small individual struggle into the wider world of the imaginal and symbolic language. These symbols and images speak to us every day from the outside world, and often collective images have the power to release in us great feeling. Images of the huge, soulful eyes in the beautiful children of Rwanda needed no words to speak to us but became symbols of innocence trapped in slaughter. Images of the dignified procession of robed Kurds making their weary, hungry way into the mountains having been hunted out of Iraq, became the powerful symbol of unfair marginalization and invited deep feelings. And so it is with the symbols of hero and heroine, prince and princess, magical saviour, potent advocate.

Try the following exercise. Find a quiet place and settle down with pen and paper. Write down what comes to you when you ask yourself the following questions.

- What is your image of being on the edge?
- What is its geography, landscape, feel, smell, sound?
- Is there anyone or anything there with you?
- Does this image remind you of anything?
- What does this image tell you?

We will return to working with the image in Part Two. For now, just let the image itself offer you information from day to day. Let it tell you about itself. Allow yourself to have a dialogue with it, checking in every other day to see if anything has changed. This need not be hard work. Think of it as a way of checking blood pressure or temperature. It is in fact a recording of the situation of your innermost life.

Margaret's image of being on the edge was standing alone on a ledge near the top of a high cliff in a freezing gale wearing only a thin cotton dress. She was standing holding on to some scrub grass, afraid that the ledge would break, and there was nothing between it and the ocean below. She had always been terrified of water. She had not learned to swim and hated to get wet. She believed that if she fell into the water she would either be drowned or dashed against the rocks. To help her secure her position on the cliff face she imagined a pair of fulmars which had made their nest nearby. They befriended her and helped to secure her to the ledge by building it up in strength, so that she could stay as long as was needed to make a decision about her position. She was very fond of birds and they had come to her rescue at other times. Fulmars are members of the gull family. They are loyal and protective, and can scale heights and soar great escarpments without flapping their wings. Their help gave her time to look down into the water below with safety.

When she looked more deeply at the nature of water, getting wet, feeling water all around her with the risk of being pulled under into an ocean depth, she began to weep. She associated her weeping with a huge ocean of feeling inside her belly. In time she connected this ocean feeling with the loss of her mother when she was four. She watched her aunts weeping whilst she sat dry-eyed as the 'good little Daddy's girl'. She had made the decision early on to be the controlled good girl who never cried or had deep feelings, for fear of being in the 'nowhere world' of feeling and being washed away.

What had taken her to this place she felt was the ending of a long relationship with a lover. The relationship had been dreary and lacked energy for some time, but neither had been able to end it. They were unable to mourn for the loss of what had gone and move on. She had felt suspended in the relationship for the last two years, until her partner had one day announced that he was about to move in with someone else. It was totally unexpected and the next day she was left with a half-empty flat which was too big for her and a terror of falling.

Once she was able to work with her image she was able to begin to get just a little wet with feeling and to allow herself, with help and containment from therapy, to be awash with the unresolved grief for her mother, as well as her most recent relationship. In connecting with her more feeling side, coming to value it rather than live in dread of it, she was able to let go in other feeling situations, to allow feeling to enrich her inner life as well as her communication with other people.

One man experienced his edge as being a narrow path in a dark valley in between two rocks. The edge was long-lived as he struggled with the melancholy of depression, with the dark of despair, whilst he accepted the shadow of the mountains on either side.

> Late, by myself, in the boat of myself
> no light and no land anywhere,
> cloudcover thick. I try to stay
> just above the surface, yet I'm already under
> and living within the ocean.
>
> Rumi, 'Saladin's Begging Bowl'

What Does the Image Mean?

The image we have of being on the edge will hold much information about different aspects of ourselves, the place we find ourselves in and the journey we are to make. As we look into it further and contemplate it more deeply we will find dimensions we had not considered before. Take for example the image of the humble onion and the spiral this creates. If we were to have the image of an onion we might think it a rather ordinary, basic and somewhat dull one. But the following steps could show us a different picture.

1 *Focusing.* Look carefully at the onion in the image – *your* onion. Concentrate on its details, the actual size, shape,

27

colour, smell, texture, the setting in which it is placed, the time of day, the light around it, anything else that appears in the image. Any detail we can bring to the actual setting in which our image is placed helps to bring it more sharply into focus.

This process is like focusing the lens on a special camera that will show us the depths of something.

2 *Personal association.* Then we move on to ponder on our personal associations with the image, in our example the onion we have now focused upon in minute detail. What is this onion like for us, what do we associate with this image? For example: it makes me cry when peeling; I use it in all cooking, it adds flavour to things; it makes my breath smell; it grows in winter in my neighbour's garden, or at the railway allotments; I don't like onions much; my Gran had a bun like an onion. These are our first impressions and our personal associations with the image of the onion.

3 *What does the image remind me of?* If we were to ask when we were first aware of the onion, we might evoke a memory such as helping Gran to peel an onion to make a stew; wielding a spade on a frosty morning to help Mum to dig them up in the garden; carrying a bag of onions home by bike; seeing a French onion-seller with a string of them on his bicycle; Uncle Joe's prize onions at the vegetable competition; harvest festival onions; the street market and baskets of onions; being shown the number of inner rings within the onion when it is sliced open, the pinkish flesh when the outer wrapping is stripped away, counting the rings; or dipping half an onion into ink and making a print for a birthday card. And each of these reminders from the past will carry an evocation of feeling. I felt sad, happy, in awe; I heard singing, sighing, the robin; I was alone, with others, with an important person for me; and, deeper in meaning, this was the first time I had been allowed to help, to use a knife, to do something on my own, perhaps even the first time I saw a grown-up cry.

4 *Amplification.* Then in a wider context the symbol of the onion shape is used in the sacred domes of mosques and orthodox churches, it is a central Indian design. It is often seen as a symbol of unity, the many in the one, the cosmos, revelation, peeling off layers to reach the centre, and is used to help

baleful lunar powers in pagan tradition. It is also a root and linked with the earth and all the qualities of the earth as it grows silently within the dark of the earth's womb.

If we stay with whatever has emerged from this short four-point exercise, what kind of information emerges? In applying this knowledge and awareness to our own individual life, what does this mean for us? That we are being invited to inspect the image of the onion and its layers, perhaps seeing and naming the different layers until we come to the actual core or heart inside. What is the heart or core that we are being asked to meet right now? This process can be applied in working with all images.

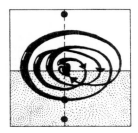

3

What Might We Become?

EGO, SELF AND SOUL

The analytical psychologist Carl Jung believed that at the beginning of life, at the point of the quickening of life inside the womb, was the seed within the growing foetus of our own unique individual self. This unique self is connected to the personal life of the human family with its biological genes and social and cultural heritage, to our own individual myth, and also to the collective unconscious. In order to survive and communicate in the everyday outside world, every individual needs to develop a container, called ego, through which the individual personality expresses itself, and within which the developing self is protected whilst links between the ego and the self are strengthened. A strong, healthy ego–structure helps to hold and withstand the powerful energies of the inner self especially when it makes links with the larger, collective force of the Self. And it is through the work of the ego that we are able to make images conscious and connect with their variety and meaning. Ego also has edges to watch out for. When the edges of the ego become too rigid and we live only in that realm we become too fixed and limited, cut off from the many powers of the self to help us grow wise. And if the edges of the ego are too undeveloped they can be weak and porous and we may be flooded with unconscious uncontained images and feeling forces which sweep us over the edge of conscious containment and safety as in schizophrenia and psychosis.

Reaching maturity and wisdom demands an inner journey that promotes the flexible dance between the ego and the self. This journey moves through the early childhood and adolescence stages of ego strengthening and development as a person moves from nursery into the outside world, through adulthood to a mid-point of life where the differentiation between ego and self is at its most extreme. The 'mid-life crisis' frequently heralds a call from the self to govern the journey of the second half of life. True maturity and wisdom emerge from the enfoldment of the ego–personality into the service of the self, with the note and way of the self becoming clearer as it moves us along the path for which our original seed was intended, and to take up our individual myth and purpose. Today, many people are reaching this 'mid-life crisis' point in their late twenties, and again in their early forties.

The seed of our whole being will be attuned potentially to the many layers of our own unique individual 'onion': to the ego–personality which is the outer layer and protects the inner rings; to the inner layers which reveal our capacity to express ourselves in our true individual way and in soulful terms, and to live a spiritual life; and to those layers that connect us with our individual myth, and in a wider sense to the familial and archetypal patterns which will be constellated throughout our life. The latter may be referred to as *karma* in Hindu and Buddhist cultures. *Karma* is a useful concept meaning archaic remnants from other times, the baggage – emotional, physical or actual – from other experiences lived by the soul dimension. When *karma* 'ripens', we experience a mixture of our woundedness, our shadow side and the intense feeling that another hand is at work in our life. When we work through *karma*, or forge a new understanding when we are brought to the edges of ourselves, we leave it behind in that particular form. We may well have to encounter it again as the spiral of life presses us on both our wound and our individual myth, and each time we have the opportunity for growth and receiving wisdom.

Choosing to embrace the possibility for a soul dimension means that we deepen our life from event into experience. Soul is one of the most potentially powerful and meaningful images humans can embrace. Soul can be seen as a root metaphor for the great dance and potentially transcendent drumbeat of life for all living creatures and countries, and for the world itself. It is used widely throughout the world, in and out of a religious context. In our language we speak of 'soulful' to describe a piece of music that moves us beyond the explanation of rational wording. A nation can seem to be suffering a 'soul sickness' as in the tearing apart of Yugoslavia and Rwanda. We can speculate about the soul sickness in Ireland, as its heart is constantly rent in two by opposing religious and political forces and it suffers the second highest incidence of death from heart disease.

We see something of the 'soul' through the eyes of children and animals, and in particular those who are suffering. It seems that profound human experiences touch us on a soul level, inviting us into something beyond our everyday awareness and control. The opportunity for making a connection with soul are everywhere and every day, for soul is both a deepening and usually connected to something quite simple. We can experience soul in moments of great love or religious awe, in deep sadness and suffering, in moments of peak or transcendent experience when we feel at one with the universe and connect with the beauty and magnificence of universal love. Sometimes it can seem that only through suffering can our soul shine through. This may be because it is usually the ego–self that experiences suffering first, that feels it has lost face or status, that is hurt by rejection and loss, that feels marginalized. Once we can step aside from the suffering to the ego we are more able to receive the soul's wisdom on the meaning of our suffering and how we are to live it. This process allows us to be as close to our own real nature and to the God within us as we can possibly come, so that we can really hear and respect the note of our own soul.

Soul can easily become eclipsed by the everyday world when we are rushing about to get somewhere, catch the bus, fix a meal, earn money, fight with each other. But soul is still there, and it is always, as James Hillman writes, 'in the thick of things, in the repressed, the shadow, in the messes of life, in illness and in the pain and confusion of love'.

People near the end of their life are often said to be more in contact with their soul–nature as they become wise and have less need of ego–gratification. Connecting with soul by means of communication with the transpersonal self (that which goes beyond) can widen and deepen our range of thinking and feeling to include a profound transcendence of understanding. This can help us journey beyond the known to forge a strong connection with soul and come closer to a true religious attitude.

WOUNDING

All of us are wounded in some way. The word 'wounding' and the concept of the wound are very evocative. Many of us can identify exactly where we feel wounded – we hold our hand at our throat, we draw in a breath, we rub our stomachs, we arch our backs, we press the palms of our hands on our hearts. Words, situations outside, smells, feelings, sounds, and simple questions asked in kindness can press us on a tender place, reminding us. We may not know its full nature in the literal sense, but we do know that we must carry this wound and tend it. And the spiral of life will pass over it, sometimes in ways that merely flutter, but may press hard, feel too close, threaten to open it up or plunge straight at it. How we carry this sense of woundedness matters. Accepting the wound, making it ours rather than someone else's fault – even if some aspect of it was inflicted by another originally – means making a relationship with all that we are. It is a relief to know our wounds, to know that some things really are difficult or impossible, not just due to our lack of willpower. To accept woundedness and start from there frees us from having to search endlessly for 'perfection' – whatever that is! Sometimes we can get caught up in imagining that therapy will cure all and we will return to innocence, to the Garden of Eden that we imagine childhood should have been. Or we may spend years looking for the mother and father we never had, but in the outside world rather than inside ourselves. Relating fully to what has happened to us means allowing the expression of the wound in all its blues, purples and reds, and finding healing ways of addressing the wound. This may involve working at understanding fully the patterns of our early life and in particular at the old survival mechanisms we have learned which may now be limiting our development. There is no point in behaving as if we are still being chased by a tiger when the jungle atmosphere has in fact diminished. All of us at some time in our lives need to take stock of where we have come from and look afresh at the motivations for the things we do. Usually we need to let go of the habit of attachment to past suffering and what helps this is a revision of past coping styles. Therapy can be extremely helpful for this process, so can reading and talking with trusted others about how we feel. This process may involve our making different kinds of relationships, with others, and most certainly within ourselves where we try out expressing ourselves differently. When we are on the edge we are closest to our woundedness and our fragility.

SHADOW

Shadow literally means 'that which is not in the light'. The shadow of a human personality contains all the aspects that have not been recognized. There are always shadow aspects, and to be cut off from our shadow is to be alienated and one-dimensional. This is well described in *Peter Pan*, when Peter is unable to be himself until Wendy sews his shadow back on. There has been a tendency in recent years to deny the aspect of the shadow we fear and to search only for the light. Any psychology, religion or system of meaning that does not make space for the shadow aspects of life encourages these aspects to fester and grow bigger in the darkness. The whiter we make Christ in Christian cultures the blacker becomes the Devil. The more we put energy into being 'good' and sharpen our swords against bad, the more likely evil will be manifest. The Breakthrough hexagram 43 of the *I Ching* reads:

> If evil is branded it thinks of weapons, and if we do it the favour of fighting against it blow by blow, we lose in the end because thus we ourselves get entangled in hatred and passion.

Perhaps it is getting easier for us to take on board that as humans we have within us the capacity for both good and evil because evidence of darkness and what collectively we have called evil is so manifest in our world: ethnic fighting in Rwanda and Yugoslavia, violence, rape and torture across the globe. It is not new that human behaviour can be cruel and evil, but we now have so much documented evidence that it places upon us the responsibility of having to take a view and find a choice of how we deal with the shadow. Some of the events that have come to light over the last ten years have made us face just how dark human beings can be: the Aids epidemic, the evidence of widespread child sexual abuse within families and child prostitution have forced us to think about what it means to be a sexual being and how we use this energy. The massacres at Port Arthur and Dunblane have forced us to look at the emotional consequences for people who become marginalized in our culture but, unlike the official holders and trumpeters of the edge such as travellers and Gypsies, have found no place to go other than into the deepest recesses of the dark edges.

Within us the shadow is like a great compost heap, full of discarded matter as well as unknown depths. It both festers and encourages new growth. It is by connecting with figures, feelings and aspects of the shadow that we are most likely to grow and become wise. But the shadow is not just for integration. It is to be respected as a dimension that always sobers any idea we might have that we have got things all together. Wholeness, as I said at the beginning, is accepting both sun and shadow. When we live on the edge we are closest to our personal darkness and most vulnerable to the shadow figures who may beckon us from their shadowy places and even take us with them for a while, into the depths, into madness, into behaviours that shock and appal, repel and seduce, into the places furthest from the light. And it is in this place that we get to know our darkest nature best and develop an appropriate awe for the energy that has come calling.

A TRANSPERSONAL PERSPECTIVE

The experience of the transpersonal perspective allows us to see beyond everyday consciousness, which is the domain of the ego, to a deeper and more enduring sense of self and the collective. Peak experience, depth experiences of awe, wonder, numinosity and light, out-of-body and psychic phenomena, dreams, near-death experiences, are all examples of experiences that transcend our everyday awareness that are called transpersonal. They include but transcend the everyday 'I'. Transpersonal experience

35

forges a bridge between ego and self so that the demand of each may be heard and understood. In this way we are enabled to move past the edges of consciousness and ego and what we have known before, and create new links with other parts of our mind and being.

We can create links with the transpersonal self which we find both in transcendent states associated with the higher consciousness and in the deepest, darkest aspects of our being when all consciousness has been abandoned, when we have broken down and given up. Transpersonal psychology therefore seeks to bring this dimension of spirit and soul, of a human capacity to move beyond the known into deeper personal meaning and transcendence, into the work of psychology, offering us a larger canvas for understanding our journey of life. If psychology only looks at individuals as being the sum total of their given psychological labels, such as neurotic, psychotic, paranoid, anorexic, it leaves behind the image of a person as an individual traveller and mythmaker with their own context, story and unique thumbprint. A transpersonal perspective can widen our listening capacity and our heart and mind connection to many different concerns of life; it is not limited to psychology. In a recent article in *The Psychologist*, David Fontana and Ingrid Slack write:

> At all levels and in all societies, transpersonal experiences and beliefs can affect human relationships, life philosophies, reactions to death and bereavement, education, and responses to economic hardship and natural disasters. A major feature of transpersonal psychology is its conviction that the psychologies of the Eastern and Western worlds have much to offer each other. The scientific approach of the West, with its emphasis upon objectivity and exploration turned outwards, and the contemplative approach of the East, with its emphasis on self-exploration, have the potential to cross-fertilize each other in a number of important areas.

Connecting with a transpersonal self means connecting with a self that knows what it is doing, even when the everyday 'I' does not. This can be called upon to show us the way to link with past, present and future. This is the self that can be the most active influence in our lives; that keeps us in touch with a sense of spiritual presence, spiritual awakening, meaning, reaching out to others. The belief that the transpersonal dimension actually has us, not that we have it, means that we are humbled to take note of all that happens to us and to the invitations life brings to take us to new understanding.

Throughout this book, as we look at the journey on, in and through the edge, we will be journeying with a transpersonal perspective. My hope is that you will find your own transpersonal note within you and begin to connect with this note, for it to be the soul caller and guide throughout all of life. As a general guide, the hallmarks of a transpersonal perspective are as follows:

- to attend to each moment and the note, feeling and image it brings forth
- to listen with the inner, poetic ear, inviting the note of the soul to express itself
- to learn to dance to the music of the soul as we experience it in ourselves and recognize it within others and the world
- to know that everything has potential for meaning, the meaning that we give it even when we cannot fully see it at the time
- to connect equally with both the journey of the ego–personality and that of the self, to become aware that both are part of a spiritual and soulful journey, that a meaningful life and spiritual journey are not limited to religious organizations or to a life lived in spiritual isolation
- to know that solitude is necessary for the development of listening, but relating is necessary for growing, and that love, beauty, laughter, and joy are food for nourishing the soul dimension
- to know the difference between the voice of the ego–personality and the voice of the self that has us
- to make an offering to the wider, greater transpersonal forces and energies that move within us and around us so that this link is kept aflame.

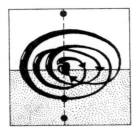

4

Mapping the Two Journeys of Life

Life cannot be lived in a linear, preprogrammed way. It is not a logical progression like a school or university calendar. Human beings evolve and journey throughout their lifespan, cultivating, processing, inhabiting, culturing different aspects of themselves according to the forces that come from both without and within. It is the transpersonal contribution, as we saw in Chapter 3, to view each of us as born with an individual DNA, the seed of our being, the person we are destined to be in the life we find ourselves born to. This force of destiny is not something laid down and written in stone. It is a continual weaving process made by the extraordinary dance of the seed of our being inside, the personality we carry into the world and the patterns of both the individual and the collective world we are born into. The individual seed with which we come into life carries genetic history, personality, archetypal patterns, and something uniquely ours called self, which is able to transcend the limits of personality and link us to the greater and collective Self.

Parts of us tend to develop more fully than others and at different rates, and I have already mentioned the difference between the self we have adapted to be to suit our environment and the 'seed' self we bring into life. We are also all permeable to the unexpected, and many of us by the time we reach our early twenties, if not before, will have an inner sense that some hand is at work within us that is not of our own doing.

THE SPIRAL MAPS

Maps help to give us a guide as to where we might be heading and help us to see where we have come from. If we fall into an alien place and do not know the geography, a map gives us some bearings. But however complete the map, it always carries the thumbprints of the mapmaker and it may take some time before it makes any sense to us personally. There are, however, certain landmarks that are so outstanding they are unquestionable. The ocean, water tower, forest or main highway, for example, are clear markers in the external geography that help us to locate the patch of land upon which we are sitting. Birth, childhood, school, friendships, deaths, illnesses, siblings, home, travel, university, children, marriage, relationships and jobs are all outside land-marks in the life of an individual. But what might the maps be that help us to see where we might be in terms of our inner life, or for our life as a whole, the maps which show where we have come from, where we are now and where we might be going to, maps which will show our journey in progress from both inside and out, so that we may gather the threads of each as some sort of measurement or checkpoint in the gathering of our bearings?

Maps are especially important when we have reached a place of the edge and we are uncertain where to go next and what is around the corner of our edge. Although the map itself is not the country, it can offer a useful and potent image for us to draw strength and imagination from. It can be of immense comfort in times of great uncertainty. It helps dignify our loss and suffering and can offer us the courage to travel on, with the map as our guide and compass.

Psychology has offered many different maps over the last hundred years to help travellers make sense of their inner land-scape and the journey they might make throughout one lifetime. But no one map can encompass the complex structure of a person's personality, self and lifespan. The following series of spirals attempt to map cycles of our life and the possible dance between the ego and the self as they emerge in tandem through-out our life development. The spiral is an image I keep turning to as a way of making sense of how life repeatedly returns us to similar places. It reminds us that we return to that which calls us: our myth, our journey, our path, our way, our *karma*, and the invitation to place this experience within the whole. The spiral's constant weaving round means a movement on and away and up or down, but the central core of the spiral remains the same. It remains a constant focus to come back to as we evolve and as the spiral demands our movement into and around it. The spiral may swing wide when we feel we are separate from the core; it may bend deep into the core when we are pulled again into the realm of the self and to our deepest, innermost places.

The interface between ego and self is the place where unconscious and conscious aspects of life meet together. The interface is the stage upon which the drama of our psychological life is played. Here at the interface we meet our dreams and fantasies, archetypal figures, images from the soul life, calls from the spirit; here we meet the thrust of the self that has something in mind for us.

The Beginning Spiral

Here we have an image of the relationship between ego and self from the time before and after we are born and for those first nursery years until we attend school and begin to negotiate the outside world. Self and ego are merged together within the body and the unconscious world of whoever was mother for us. We may have had an actual mother or a stream of different mothers, or a father, uncle, grandmother or sister may have acted as mother for us. But whoever took on that early role plays an important part in shaping our experience of ourselves, both the ego–self and the seed–self. No other period of brain learning and physical growth is as significant as this period.

Humans emerge at birth as more helpless than any other beings in the animal kingdom, and their early years after birth are crucial to their development. The task of these early years is for external independence to develop: walking, sleeping, eating, the physical command of body functions, language mastery and communication skills. Internally, we need the ego to begin to emerge in its own right by the time we go out into the world of other people, and for our sense of seed–self to take root within us. Whatever is our own true nature will always try to assert itself. Our traits, our likes and dislikes, our gifts, our pleasures, our capacities, our ease with our own bodies, our expression of feelings, our way of thinking and our connection with the transpersonal self, all take root to greater or lesser extent during these important years.

These different aspects of our original seed will be seen, perhaps noted and commented upon, by others. This is vitally important because it means that we are being mirrored by others. We hope that we are mirrored as we really are, not as others wish us to be. Too much mirroring in another's image can send us looking endlessly for our real reflection in all the wrong places. But no mirroring at all would probably be worse. We often find, when we look back on old photographs of our childhood, that we see something of our real, original selves in the little figures, before the mask of adaptation hid our seed from outside view. Many people are able to connect with images of 'otherness' that began during childhood: a special image, an imaginary friend or place, a sense of presence, a particular affinity with nature – with stones, rivers, birds, trees, plants and animals, an imaginary inner landscape, a favourite toy, an object, a dream. If for any reason the path of our natural growth is halted, such as when we suffer early separation or bereavement, or when we experience a restricted, conditional, cruel or abusive early life, we adapt accordingly. If this movement involves some rejection of or separation from our own true seed–nature, there will be a wound inflicted, and at some time in the future, this wound will draw us back for the purpose of reparation.

Sometimes when we are on the edge we experience images and feelings that take us back to an earlier part of life – a sense of helplessness, for example, or an inability to express ourselves in words. Some people may feel childlike, as fragile and unprotected as they once felt as a small child, or they may feel persecuted, trapped, judged and discriminated against, as they did early in life. And whilst these experiences may be real, it is important as adults to address the *feelings* we carry inside, and how these feelings are still informing the decisions and choices we make in our daily lives. When part of us feels judged, we will always be vulnerable to others' perceived judgements and we may act as harsh judges of ourselves. An earlier rejection sets up the antici- pation of further rejections. These feelings remain hidden until forced into our consciousness. The wound Margaret suffered over the loss of her mother (*see* Chapter 2) had remained

41

unaddressed until her adult relationship ended. None of us can go back and undo what happened to us and we cannot spend our lives looking for the perfect mother or father we never had. But once we are conscious of these things, we *can* become kind and wise midwives to ourselves, going back in time to heal old wounds and making a conscious decision to choose not to be limited by what has gone before. We can in fact use what has happened to us to link with our individual myth and archetypal pattern, so that we grow in our wisdom and understanding and widen our compassion.

Those people who are now having to relive their wound of abuse from childhood seem to be doing so amid a collective awareness of the fact of childhood abuse. We all have the choice whether to see this wounding only literally and seek literal and legal revenge, or to mobilize our outrage, shock and horror and move towards a wider embrace of all the aspects to this suffering, which spreads back into generations of families and their unhappy terrible secrets. This devastating woundedness would then be carried by us all; it would demand that we all open our hearts and minds to what is possible within the human family and bring us to honour the need for making conscious that which in the past has only been able to be borne by darkness. It might move us to be fully conscious, and pay attention to all our negotiations and relationships so that they move into the realm of the power of love, rather than the love of power.

The Child Spiral

The second spiral refers to the stages of the development of the ego from out of the nursery years and mothering presence, and tends to refer to the period from around the age of five until the beginning of adolescence. This period involves the ego–strengths becoming more consolidated as the young individual learns about authorities other than his or her parents and hears other voices and opinions. During this stage the functions of thinking and feeling begin their process of development, as we experience relationships outside the family and have to deal with our own response, and not be carried by the emotional world of parents.

Our sense of real or seed–self may be more fully consolidated during these years as we extend our time of play and growth, develop different skills, make friends and take our place within the family. It may be during these years that inner edges emerge, and the beginning of our personal capacities sharpen themselves because of the demands of outside life.

The Spiral of Adolescence

This is a time of emerging ego, when it needs to be strong enough to withstand the great changes going on within and the call to move away from parental bonds and find apprenticeship with the clan in the outer world. In adolescence we often begin to hear the earlier drumbeats of our own seed–nature and to connect consciously with our individual myth. This occurs at a time of great pressure from outside to conform, to grow up, to take on the challenges of the world, to develop an identity in order to appear in the world and the workplace. We often take on paths at this time because of immediate need rather than reflective attitude. It is a time when new tunes are being tried out alongside the pressure to either do or be. The interface here becomes that space where the developing ego meets both parents and other authorities with different voices. It is a time when the parental voice is challenged, often thrown over completely for a time, and other voices and forms of authority are chosen. Young people then develop their own heroes and heroines, tribes, clans with their own systems of meaning, their own dress, music and forms of affection, away from parental influence.

This is a period of great experimentation, of intense feelings of death and rebirth, as the person moves from girl to woman, boy to man. The rituals of this time are those of the peer group, the campfire, music-making and the exchange of talismans and dress. It is a time for the parental influences to drop back and other authorities to take root. It is a dangerous and exciting rite of passage when the longings to get high, to find a transcendent self, to get above materialism and into idealism and flight are at their most compelling. The ego needs to be strong for the emerging self to express its values and its path. And the depths of experimentation can seem extremely dangerous today. To push to the edge of one's parental limits was once to stay out late, drink too much or have one's ears and nose pierced. Today finding an individual edge away from authority can involve joy-riding, drug abuse, stealing, even killing, as if the imagination has taken wings and gone beyond itself in the literal sense. For all these adolescent excursions and diabolic routes, what is it that is being imagined, hoped for, transcended?

Adulthood Spiralling

The fourth spiral shows the ego and the self at their furthest apart. It is as if the ego has grown as much as it can and fulfilled its tasks, and that its time begins to be up. It has gone as far as it possibly can and the further dimensions of self need to move into prime position. This is often a time in life when the voice of the self really begins to be heard in the most compelling way. Crises of ego/self differentiation always include an experience where the ego begins to experience death. Since we feel our life through the ego this can be extremely shattering. There may actually be a death which takes us to the edge, or the threat of death; it may be the death of an important relationship, a job, a belief in a cause or a deeply held faith. We may fail at something, which can feel like death to the ego, and for a while we may feel we are lost in the darkness, not knowing where next to turn.

This point of feeling the ego to be so completely separate from the self may be arrived at earlier, when we feel alienated from anything meaningful but yet do not have the strength to cope. When we have held all life's energy within our ego–personality this part of us can become inflated. It begins to think it has all the answers, that it is God himself. This is a dangerous situation because the energies of the self are powerful and need a strong but humbled ego with dynamic boundaries through which to transmit its numinosity. (Ken Wilbur emphasizes that a spiritual journey requires a strong ego to withstand the power of the self with its numinosity and invitation to meet the brightest of lights and the darkest of dark places.)

Mature Spiral

Here the inner spiral is moving in again to be closer to the self in order to begin to be of service to it. Maturity is having had the kind of life experiences that make us realize that the 'I' of the ego–personality is not actually in charge, nor does it offer us the whole picture of who we really are; some essence far greater is at work. We may be worn and a bit jaded, but a sparkle has begun to glow in our eyes and there is a spring in our step. We may not know clearly what we want, but we know what we do not want. We may have had many different jobs and relationships but we are ready for something 'other', we are ready to sniff around hidden crevices we have seen before but not investigated. This is often a time when books seem to fall off shelves at us, friends tell of some mystery, or we hear the songs of birds or the note of music in a new, deeper way. These things may well have, and probably have, always been there, but we see them with fresh eyes and their quality moves deeper into us. We may well also have consolidated our energy into our life's journey with a deep sense of meaning. We feel we are onto something, onto an adventure of far greater excitement than we could have envisaged when we were in adulthood, living out a one-dimensional life.

Maturity seems to be connected to being able to live in the present and relish every moment whilst guiding the different aspects of one's personality into the future and not dwelling too much on the past. There are sadnesses rather than regrets, acceptance rather than resignation, a half-full glass rather than one which is lamented as half-empty. We know the limits of our own ego and its tendency to try and rise up and we deal with it with humour, maybe bashing it down from time to time or laying it to one side so that other elements may rise, either within us or in younger people around us. We have accepted that we are simply not in charge and surrendered ourselves to a higher order at the same time as holding the thread of what has been important in our lives and for our own individual journeys. During maturity we come to have a greater sense of ego being overlapped by the self and move on to submit ourselves to the will of the self in the stage of wisdom.

45

The Spiral of Wisdom

Here the spiral returns to its original shape after a life's journeying. We come into wisdom after we have journeyed through the twists and turns of the spiral and met our individual psychological need to move through all the stages of growth. Wisdom means truly knowing the dance between ego and self. In wisdom the realm of the self and the collective archetypes are prime and we become open to the higher aspects of our transpersonal being and its gifts, a filter passing on from within us to others. A wise person has known the struggles, pains and losses of life and remained connected to joy and peace; he or she can affirm the strength of the masculine principle and use it for focus and command and true authority, and weave with the finest of feminine principle threads.

MEETING OF OPPOSITES

Many of us emerge into adulthood with a divided sense of our choices of how to be. We feel we must be 'either/or' and 'if . . . then'. Throughout this book we will be looking at different aspects of polarized choices and how we can come into working more with the 'and . . . and' philosophy, in order that we might move into a third position that does not split us in two and leave us stranded on the edge of tension between the two.

One of the most severe polarizations in human life has been that between the qualities of masculine and feminine energies. Jung referred to masculine and feminine as the archetypes of anima and animus, widening the context in which we approach them way beyond the gender issues of male and female. These archetypal energies are vital for the creation of life. The Chinese philosophies refer to them as the principles of *yin* and *yang*. Some males carry more feminine energy than masculine and some women carry more masculine energy. The qualities of each are necessary for all life but a new relationship with the feminine principle has particular importance today as we are moving from the dominance of the more masculine consciousness into a realignment with the feminine. For this energy to be aligned equally means that it becomes the vital conjoint, the aspect that speaks to ecology, to beauty, to the force behind relationship and to the power of love rather than the love of power.

LIFE-CYCLE EXERCISE

Imagine that inside yourself, within the seed of the self, there is the music of the soul. Every five to seven years a gong or drumbeat sounds as if to move you on to the next phase of your being, the next phase of your unfolding. Make a lifeline for yourself marking the significant events, feelings, attitudes and changes that occurred around the ages of five to seven. Then do the same for the ages of 12–14 then 19–21, then 26–28 and so on every five to seven years. It often happens that changes begin to occur at around the five-year period to encompass the actual shift by the seven-year mark. You might like to take up the theme that is contained in your image of the edge and follow the development of this theme throughout your life. If – as in Margaret's case – it is connected with water and feelings, trace these elements and their nature throughout the cycles in your own individual and particular way.

Part Two

PROPERTIES OF THE EDGE

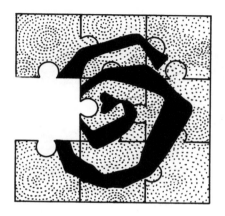

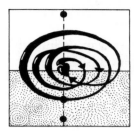

5

Preparing to Explore the Edge

Chapters 6–14 map nine properties of the edge. Each has its own landscape, history, feeling quality, associations and both light and darkness. The maps attempt to chart and describe what it is like actually to be immersed in the property for a period of time: weeks, months, perhaps years. The maps also attempt to chart a loose guide to being there and offer some thoughts on how we might bear the psychological tension by the pull of opposites. Each property will be unknown to us when we first move into that place and therefore new and frightening. Most people's experience of time spent on the edge is one of long, monotonous, miserable and worrying tension, with extremes of feeling and a constant fear of going over the edge into darkness.

There will also be potentially positive aspects as well as pitfalls and dangers as we explore the nature of each place. Negotiating the edge can be an opportunity to harness powerful inner energies and to break through to something new, and it can also mean an encounter with pitfalls that result in our falling into our personal chasm. How we experience ourselves being on the edge, what it provokes within us, what it invites us to fight or to dance among, all become part of the journey we make. It is a soul-forging experience, the dimension of which we will not see clearly until we are able to get some distance from the edge itself. This forging process is the crucial element in our whole journey and affects its outcome. If we do not engage with what is happening to us and never move away from our first reaction to the dangerous new, we remain stuck, or hang in limbo; or we may be swept away by the very forces we are trying to resist. At the edge we are also prey to false prophets who entice us one way or the other and seem to offer relief, but may lead us into the blind alley of illusion, addiction or suicidal impulse. It may be that encounters with false prophets are actually part of the journey we need to make, but we need something of a guide to allow us to make the wisest judgements and selection and not stumble blindly and passively on, unable to read the warning signs. It may be that a period of feeling stuck or in limbo or being in the blind alley of addiction becomes the very enlightening experience that brings home to us the seriousness of our predicament. The aim of a map or chart is to help us see the kind of landscape we are likely to encounter and prepare as best we are able. Sometimes the map does not become really alive until after we have visited the place. Then it serves as a powerful record of the extent of our travels and offers a useful reminder and record.

Having examined the properties of the edge we may choose to stay there, recognizing it as the place where we live best. But our choice then is an informed and conscious one rather than an avoiding or lazy refuge.

And for people whose lives are defined by the edge because of their extreme personal encounters with badness, hardship, mindless violence or long-term painful physical or mental abuse and illness, the greatest triumph may be surviving to live on the edge of their bleak universe and not letting it destroy them.

Each of the nine properties of the edge contain the potential for both breaking through and for breaking down. True breakthrough always involves the process of breaking up to break down in order to break through. We have to allow a death in order to make way for a birth. Breaking through is going on at the same time as breaking down. In *Suicide and the Soul* James Hillman writes:

> The death motif is always present at the beginning of change and appears in order to make way for transformation. The creative force kills as it produces the new. The flower withers around the swelling pod. The snake sheds its skin.

Breakup is usually experienced most painfully by the ego–personality where it hurts the most. Identifying the aspect that is most engaged with the suffering of breakup means naming what it is we feel we are losing. It could be control, for example, but we need to ask: control of what? Identity could suffer, so we need to be asking with what or whom we have identified ourselves. Over-all questions when exploring the maps of the edge are: what is it within me that needs most to undergo change? Which function – thinking, feeling, intuition, sensation – is most involved in this process of change? Which aspect of myself has perhaps been over-valued and which undervalued? An individual question is: what part of me, my behaviour or my attachments, is most at stake right now? It may be the least-known part of us which suffers. In breakup and breakdown we always find ourselves in a situation where nothing that has gone before helps us to cope. We are in the midst of something completely new and therefore alien, we are unpractised and this is what makes us feel lost.

So often in our Western culture it is the ego–functions of control, extroversion and performance that become valued and admired, with any fragility, uncertainty and woundedness rejected and repressed, or marginalized by harsh judgement. Although soul is always in evidence it is hard for it to be recognized when the hard edges of ego–control have become rigid or closed. And yet we see this polarity globally in the most vivid form. We see highly developed technology spilling its hard-edged bullets into the impoverishment of African countries, feeding the addiction to power for its own sake, for ego–gratification. Addiction to posses-sions, fashion, money, gets in the way of the wisest use of natural resources such as the earth's minerals, the oceans, the atmosphere. A Western hotel with gold bath taps rises out of a desert culture or in a large city where women, children and young people beg in the streets and waste pollutes the rivers. These extremes exist in our world and have always done so. The difference at the edge of this millennium is that we are conscious of the extremes and we have the means to address the polarities. At a recent European conference on transpersonal psychology, James Fadiman spoke of two practical acts each individual could offer as part of their enlightened living: to plant a tree and bury a gun.

SOUL–HUNGER

Many people are on the edge of their extremes or polarized choices because of a hunger for soul. They are starving for a connection to a system of meaning, to the ritual, the warmth, the love and transcendence that a life committed to a soul–dimension involves. It feels as if soul–hunger is epidemic in our culture. In individuals it rises up in the form of a longing to connect with a system of meaning, to 'come home' to something we have long left behind, to enter the 'unthought known'. Our world, the earth as well as individuals, is demanding a different kind of nourishment than ego–gratification alone has provided. The soul cannot be fed by an ego which is too fixed or rooted to being in charge, by external achievements and possessions. All the money and external power structures in the world cannot meet the place of the soul when it cries out for love.

This hunger may be the root metaphor behind the changes we are being asked to make individually and we perhaps need to refresh ourselves with the Eastern idea of meditation, that every moment counts. Recent consciousness research at Oxford has provided evidence that healing and love can be transmitted and received by another person with whom one has a connection, even between walls. If each one of us meditated upon healing at one particular time and space, who knows what the result might be. In everyday terms everything we do, think and say matters. It affects the outside world and the people in it and it certainly affects our inner living. Even the physical act of smiling has been proved to stimulate more endorphins in the brain. Leading a spiritually aware life does not mean renouncing matter and taking up a beggar's life but being aware of the impact and consequences of all that we do. The teacher who teaches from the heart, the police officer who exercises wise counsel, the shopkeeper who looks a customer in the eye while speaking, all have an impact on the general good of the soul.

Soul–hunger as it emerges into our everyday consciousness brings us more deeply in touch with our innermost self and the basis on which we have lived our lives so far. When we are committed to serve the self and listen to the voice of the soul when it speaks within us and around us in the outside world, we are ready to move along the edge, even at its narrowest places where nothing much is to be seen, and take up the patterns of a spiritual path to be our guide.

A PERSONAL TALISMAN

The dark places are all best visited by taking a thread or light to help along the way. You may wish to imagine your own talisman, something that is for you personal, special and sacred. Take some time finding an image for this with your eyes closed. Some people know immediately what special object they would wish to take as a talisman. They may already have imbued some object with special meaning, something which has seen them through previous difficult times: a stone, shell, crystal, Bible, photograph, animal or inner guide. A talisman is different from a lucky charm. It is the image which carries the energy of our inner, wise, knowing self, our transpersonal self. Sometimes what becomes a talisman is an object or image our ego–personality would not choose for aesthetic or sentimental reasons. Knowing this frees you to take the authentic energy from this place and what has been chosen for you.

IMAGINING A SAFE PLACE

Always begin any kind of inner exploration from a place of safety and return to this place after you have ventured into difficult or alien territory. This is very important when responding to the powerful images that occur when we are on the edge. Always keep an image of a safe place, and always remember to touch base with your talisman.

A safe place can be any place we know or one we find within our imaginary space. If it is hard to imagine such a place, keep coming back to the idea of safety, a safe space all of your own, whilst you are going about your everyday life. Let the image appear to you in its own time. Images for safe places have included a garden, field, river, tree, bush, room, cave or armchair – anything that offers sanctuary. Safe places may also change as we move to different aspects of the edge. If your safe place begins to change, fasten your eye on one aspect of the safety within this place and let this be your guide. Sometimes our only safe spot is in the form of a stepping stone amid a rush of water or moving ground. Grip the stone firmly with your feet or hands. If it begins to feel as if it is about to start shifting, look around for the next safe stepping stone to be your crouching or standing place. Treat the process just like a series of stepping stones; quietly step off one, once you have found another, and know that this is your anchor for the moment.

You may like to spend some time either holding an object of your choice or imagining a special place which offers you sanctuary, a place you may go back to as and when you need to.

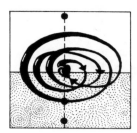

6

Chaos

The Centre that I cannot find
Is known to my unconscious mind;
I have no reason to despair
Because I am already there.

My problem is how not to will;
They move most quickly who stand still:
I'm only lost until I see
I'm lost because I want to be.

W H Auden, from 'The Maze' in *Collected Poems, 1940*

Part of being on the edge involves a return to the chaos of our once-undifferentiated state of being, but with both the curse and the joy of consciousness. Our eyes are open now, but it feels as if the ego–self is under assault and no longer in charge. We may view our choices as being only the polarity of either 'give in and let it take over ' or 'shut it out and fight it to the death'. A third position could be to follow the call to recognize that we are dealing with chaos, name the substance of it as best we can and thus invest our experience with the authority of a scientific approach. One way to meet chaos is to meet the images it brings. What is our individual image of chaos, and our relationship with that image? Chaos can represent everything we know being undone and scattered, our sense of order being in turmoil or violated. We may feel we are spinning and falling, disintegrating, fragmenting, our everyday 'I' in eclipse. Chaos can be created by the regressive pull to return to a state of unconsciousness, to feeling infantile, childlike and helpless. Our dreams and waking moments may be dominated by images of the unborn, *in utero*, in the pressure and chaotic world of the birth process, having no voice, no words, being sucked into a whirlpool or held in a vice. A brush with inner chaos is always frightening at first, partly because we have no accepted maps for this experience.

We may experience it in waves or floods, in moments, or it may come and go unexpectedly. It is experienced both inside and outside. Our internal chaos may be triggered by outside chaotic events; or we may create chaos externally because of the chaos of our internal milieu. What is chaos for one person may not be for another.

On a mundane level, many people who live ordered lives during the week, structured with work appointments and dead-lines, experience the unstructured weekend space as chaotic and seek to fill it with order or dull the anxiety chaos brings with alcohol or busyness. The opposite also occurs. A contemplative person used to enjoying a quiet life of solitude will experience noise, movement, travel, deadlines, people and busyness as having a chaotic dimension. We tend to fear chaos until we can control it, giving it a firm edge or boundary so that it cannot take us over.

When we feel on the edge, where there is not much space, any kind of chaos can seem more alarming than usual. External chaos can often be worked through by organization and planning, by negotiation, by stepping back, by waiting for the decks to clear. But when chaos seems to have crept inside us, dealing with both inside and outside can feel overwhelming. And on the edge we do not know where we are going, which in itself can feel chaotic. If we are experiencing swings of mood – feeling tearful and over-whelmed one minute, angry and hostile the next – this can feel chaotic. We just do not know where we are.

PRIMORDIAL IMAGES

Chaos is a universal fear, promoting in humans the desire for civilization and control, and initiating the erection of firm structures and buildings and the creation of containing bodies such as the church, family and government, and national

58

defences. The pleasure derived from our success in controlling vegetation by creating roads or fields offers the satisfying image of control. For nature appears chaotic and left alone it will both devour as well as nurture. The primeval forest, the ocean depths, the desert wastelands, are all primordial images that often present as chaos. Within these images are both the swirling dark depths in which we may become lost and also the seeds of systems of order that link us to patterns and rhythms of nature way beyond our wildest civilized dreams.

SHADOW SEEN AS CHAOS

When people or things viewed and feared as chaotic are repressed in consciousness and held back, they fall into the shadow areas of unconscious life, both in our individual lives and within our collective groups. Gypsies and travellers, circus people, tramps, the homeless and nomadic peoples are feared for their non-conformist attitudes, and their wild, untamed energy is viewed as antisocial. The long rule of apartheid in South Africa can be seen as an attempt by the white minority to control a larger, wider group of blacks, and keep back an energy force which they did not understand but feared as chaotic, which they believed might harm the orderly rule of the perceived controlled life. In our own individual psyches images of the tramp, wastrel, Gypsy may come to haunt us during times of chaos, especially if we have repressed the more chaotic energies of instinctual life. Conscious fears of ending life as a tramp under an embankment arch or a bag lady shuffling along in slippers often appear when we are overattached to trying to keep the edges of our civilized lives intact. Sometimes our own inner repressed energies come to us in the form of demons and devils, at night in dreams, or by day in the form of other people or causes and situations which carry the force of our projected repressed energy.

Images of chaos may include fighting in the streets, being drunk, a profusion of papers in disorder, bureaucracy taking over life, madness, a swirling cesspit, the whirlpool, the untrammelled jungle, a sailor lost at sea, feral creatures which run wild, a prostitute, a snakepit, a haunting demon. For Joseph Campbell:

Demons are our own limitations. Devil is a god who has not been recognized – the power in us to which we have not given expression and we push it back. Like all repressed energy it builds up and becomes dangerous to the position we are trying to hold.

For many civilized people the repression of sexual and instinctual energy for the sake of 'civilized order' and moral superiority causes a wound to the basic, instinctual nature from which our life-force or libido stem and our creativity merges spontaneously. Once held back for fear of its primal, chaotic nature, repressed instinctual energy may return to be claimed within us, thus pushing us to the edge of our conforming side. Jung writes that the repressed returns with knife in hand. Energies we have repressed return to claim their rights with a force that is undeniable.

THE FEAR OF CHAOS

The fear of chaos alone can lead to people clinging on to the edge, remaining firmly rooted in an outdated mode or constant state of fear. The fear is of descending back into a primal, primitive unconscious state, becoming 'like animals', and being at the mercy of a savage, untamed energy with no morality or conscious awareness. And yet if we have not been able to feel this energy consciously and know it, we cannot hold a good position with it; it remains cut off out of fear, rather than wrestled with out of respect and awe for something so mighty. And for people cut off from the potential energy of this vital force, life can feel dry, overcontrolled, unexpressive, dull, depressing, and they may take on the symptoms that animals display when captured.

The chaos most feared whilst we are on the edge is of going over the edge into breakdown. Fear of breakdown is a basic fear and may be, as D W Winnicott writes, a fear of breakdown that has already occurred earlier in life, before we became conscious. We therefore become more fearful than if we had relied on ego–energy alone to get us through. No one would choose breakdown consciously and no one would wish it on anyone else. And yet it is one overwhelming experience which, when met, and then chosen because it has chosen us, moves us into an extraordinarily deep relationship with the self. In *Breakdown*, Margaret writes:

One part of me was like a tidal wave, a disaster and I knew it couldn't hold out. Another part of me, a voice somewhere within me, would occasionally come up with a clear message, 'Suffering is privilege.' I could see that the words made sense but then something in me said, 'This is nonsense', and the tidal wave would come back. It was as though there was seed of light, or hope or strength trying to form itself.

REGRESSION

We feel as if something is pulling us back, to the place where our desire for regression is met. Returning to the womb may feel terrifying until we become aware of the nature of our rebirth. Feeling like a child – primitive, small, infantile and helpless – with all the pains of judgement of childhood experience that we also carry within us, puts us very much on the edge. We feel so little, and want to feel little, and yet there is an adult learned part which bellows at us inside, trying to stop us from feeling little. And we revisit our childhood experience and feel again put down, humiliated for our childlikeness, told to grow up, get on with it, stop showing off, stop wanting attention. Feeling like this and having an adult body is hard. Much is expected of us and often without the permissions of recognizable 'illness' this is hard to accomplish. Many people whose experience of breakdown leads them to psychiatric care speak of giving up in horror and disbelief at being in a place most feared, and then becoming like children again, with nothing expected and no responsibility within the ward. In *Breakdown* Nadia writes:

> I loved being in hospital. People think you are so mad when you like being in a psychiatric ward. In the ward there was a great deal of love with no expectations, no reservations, no judgements. I found that extraordinary. The people there meant more to me at that time than my husband and that's amazing for I've never loved anyone as much as him. But I really loved some of them. We were like children in many ways, we all had something in common and there was a tremendous amount of support, even from the most violent, aggressive people. I found it quite comforting to see people who were behaving quite wildly helping others when they were upset.

61

Van Gogh described the chaos of his plunges into melancholic despair as 'sometimes moods of indescribable anguish, sometimes moments when the veil of time and the totality of circumstances seem torn apart from an instant'. He produced huge amounts of work within the containment of hospital, expressing a liking for the order imposed. 'When I have to follow a rule, as here in hospital, I feel at peace.' The paintings of the Saint Remy period are more turbulent than those from Arles. Albert J Lubin writes in his biography of Van Gogh, *Stranger on the Earth*:

> Many are characterized by a linear style that conveys an impression of agitated movement, impulsively executed, yet with demonic control. When he recovered from the long attack of July and August he turned to self-portraits. Whilst claiming to have done so for lack of other models, he was probably trying to reconstitute himself after his disorganizing experiences.

PRIMA MATERIA

Chaos is also the *prima materia*, the original chaotic mass of substance that comes before the *logos* principle creates and names the substance of the world we know today, composed of air, earth, fire and water. Early philosophical thinking about the *prima materia* was that this original substance is only potential, without form, until the process of differentiation into elements is undertaken. The *prima materia* thus forms an archetype for all created form and for the psychological life of humans. It is out of the chaotic, undifferentiated matter of *prima materia* that form emerges via the process of separation or differentiation, naming and imagining. In *Anatomy of the Psyche*, Edward Edinger writes:

> Upon the *prima materia* was imposed, as it were, a fourfold structure, a cross, representing the four elements, two sets of contraries, earth and air, fire and water. Psychologically this image corresponds to the creation of the ego out of the undifferentiated unconscious by the process of discriminating the four functions: thinking, feeling, intuition and sensation.

The process of change within the psyche of humans can involve a return to an undifferentiated state whilst the previously dominant function is in eclipse, in order that the next unfoldment of function may emerge. Or the return to an undifferentiated state may be a natural response to a traumatic encounter, with death or loss, for example, or with violence and horror. The process of grieving can often feel like chaos. Order is abolished and rivers of grief run wild and untamed. Any form of psychological suffering can have its periods of chaos, when it feels as if the centre cannot hold and we are rendered down into a regressive state, feeling helpless and without form. From this undifferentiated childlike state we are free of ego–structure and stricture. The contents of unconscious material and images are able to flow freely through us. Given a safe place and loose structure for care, a person can undergo inner chaos and emerge changed and well.

PSYCHOSIS AND THE SELF

The most severe inner chaos is referred to in medical diagnosis as psychosis. This is a state where an individual loses touch with reality and seems lost in the unconscious world of strange voices and images often ordering him or her about in a fearful and unrelated way. Since time immemorial men and women have suffered these afflictions and needed to be cared for by family and society. In recent years what we now call mental health services have attempted to categorize such afflictions in order to decide what best to offer. At present there is no distinction in traditional psychiatric diagnosis between the mystical experience of a spiritual emergency (referred to in Stan Grof's work), creative illness, metanoic journeys, visionary states, breaking down to break through, and psychotic illness.

It seems that all mystical, unusual, non-rational growth experiences take us way into the unknown, and may also include experiences which would be diagnosed in medical terms as psychotic. There are many instances where these severe psychotic experiences are short-lived and there is a positive outcome. What seems to make a difference is the view held by the person witnessing the other's journey. If the transpersonal dimension is held for

63

the person going through the crisis period of the edge, and a self-organizing process is going on, even when it is not obvious, this can make a tremendous difference in terms of outcome.

The studies initiated by John Weir Perry in the 1950s show that in this place are manifest the seeds of the original self, showing a self-organizing principle that knows what is going on. Drawings from psychotic patients allowed to be free of medication show the use of circle or mandala symbolism. John Weir Perry's work stemmed from the time a patient suffering psychosis referred to feeling at the centre of her world. She painted a series of images and commented upon them, telling of the process of death and rebirth, the reconciling of opposites through new images, and the creation of a new cultural ideology concerned with the nature of governance. The process shifted from concerns of power and prestige to ones of lovingness and social harmony. Alongside this reporting through the paintings was her gradual recovery in terms of restored ego–consciousness and the restoration of inner order and outer relatedness. Perry's conclusion from this and other long-term studies of people undergoing psychotic experiences is that there is within each psyche an organizing process going on whose role is a self-healing one and brings about the restoration of an integrated whole.

CIRCLES AND MANDALAS

The image of the circle or mandala remains the primal symbol operating at the centre of all processes in change. Out of the circle emerges the cross, making the fourfold division, or the division of two pairs of opposites. In alchemy the steps are in four divisions designated by four colours – black, white, red and yellow or gold – resulting in the philosopher's stone which reunites the four elements. The circulating wheel image then is a powerful symbol for the process of change and transformation. The wheel needs to be kept turning in relation to the rule of all of creation, the times of spring, summer, autumn and winter. All need to have their allotted time and space and be in relationship each to the other, and in relation to the times when one is in ascendency before turning and giving way to the next. And so it

is with psychic development; the integration of the four functions of thinking, feelings, intuition and sensation requires the
wheel to be turned as each are to be developed.

CHAOS AND CREATIVITY

The nest of creativity is darkness, chaos and confusion, a nest
where we can only meet with our gods, where we are pushed to
the edge as the limit of our awareness and our capacity. Creative
work is often the result of this encounter, when out of the nest
comes a birth of something new – a new awareness, thought,
image, style, revolutionary awakening, philosophical understanding. The nest, like the alchemist's flask, is used as a womb for the
transformation of base matter – that which has gone before and
is now redundant – into something golden in its newness.

As we have seen, the *prima materia* is necessary for reclaiming
and redefining aspects of ourselves. Whilst in the experience of
chaos we will not know what these are or what they are for.
Because the experience demands that we accept and ultimately
receive the chaos into our reality, we have to surrender ourselves
consciously to it in order to be in the place where transformation
may take place. In this way we are bringing in a scientific
approach to what feels very unscientific. Receiving and allowing
do not mean that we ourselves collapse into chaos, for to do so is
to court danger. We need guides and helpers, especially when
chaos threatens to take over and the centre within us is in danger
of not holding the wheel as it turns within the furnace of the
process. Given that we do not know what we are doing or where
we are going, which is the work of the ego, we are surrendering
ego–awareness and consciousness in order to let our unconscious
show us the way. And our guide is our transpersonal self and
awareness. We allow the self that has us and knows what it is
doing to make this way clearer to us when we are ready to hear it.

When the chaotic, wild self has been directed to be tamed by
having to be 'proper', we are denied the energy of the life-force.
'Too much domestication breeds out strong and basic impulses
to play, relate, cope, rove and commune,' writes Clarissa Pinkola
Estees in *Women Who Run with the Wolves.* Artists often put

themselves on the edge by being the outsider, the recluse, the starving artist in the garret, and by internally choosing deprivation, fasting, self-abuse (drink, drugs, poisonous fumes from paint) to develop a cutting edge for their work. Any creative act involves a period of chaos and the building of a concert pitch in order to bring something together out of that chaos. Creative acts always involve non-ordinary states of consciousness.

Artists may court chaos for the purpose of getting back into an undifferentiated state. Whilst chaos can instil immediate feelings of fear and revulsion, except for those who revel in it and court it for the purpose of creativity, learning to recognize the *prima materia* can give it a different flavour. People have said of the edge, 'It goes on so long. It is grey and tedious. No one knows what it's like to suffer so, there is nothing to show for it.' This is the stuff of *prima materia*, the grit, the ordinary, the unremarkable, the leaden casket chosen by Bassanio for Portia after the suitors choosing the silver and gold had been rejected: 'You see me Lord Bassanio as I am.'

Recently whilst undergoing the chaotic aftermath of a serious illness I sat down one morning to meditate, thinking spontaneously and angrily, 'If only I could feel well.' And some voice inside me said, 'And what would you do with your wellness?' I knew that at this stage I would have taken my wellness and got back into the fast lane with it, as if that were my right. The ego–self would have been in charge once again, with its illusion of control, and I was not ready; I had not stayed long enough in the process of undifferentiation. Later, when wellness was restored after the long process of chaos, I had come to respect it and use it with much greater awareness.

DANGERS OF CHAOS

Danger comes to our potential whole if we suffer a collapse of the centre because of the inundation of unconscious ideas and images. If there is a sense of greater chaos encroaching, containment of an appropriate kind should be sought. Medication can help to hold enough of a sense of reality to keep the process of recording the images and ideas moving. Long experiences of

66

feeling chaotic are exhausting and should only be tolerated under wise supervision and when there are vehicles for anchoring the path of the self through writing, storytelling, drawing, sculpting or dancing. Chaos should only be ventured into with appropriate scientific attitudes, with a belief in the gestation chaos into the birth of a new order, new life.

EXERCISE: PATHS THROUGH CHAOS

1 Find stepping stones, however small, for the swirling sea of chaos. Stay on them until they feel as if they are in movement. Then gradually move to the next stepping stone.
2 Name the experience of chaos. Paint, sculpt, dance, sing, yell, shout, write, anchor what you experience in one of these forms, alone or shared with wise witnesses. Dignify your process by giving it form as you go along.
3 If chaos threatens to become unbearable, do not remain alone in it. Recruit helpers, wise persons, trusted clinicians, friends. If you need more than a wise midwife to your process take the help that you need: medication, safe holding, good containment.
4 Whilst recognizing chaos, dance within it, become the Dervish, take up the primordial energy and run with the wildness, move with the whirlwinds and swim with the rivers and floods, burn with the heat of fire and let your passion rise with the temperature. Fly and float and spin and do all this consciously whilst grounding yourself in the reality of your everyday life and the firmness of your stepping stone. Make the experience of chaos as full as you can possibly bear, make it your reality whilst you are in or near it. Trust its wildness to answer your bravery. Trust your honest heart to find the answers its call needs.

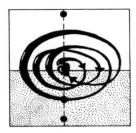

7

Exhaustion: When the Well Runs Dry

I'm tired.
From inside out
my spirit craves for
crumbs of comfort anywhere.
A body lost at sea
I sink in hopeless search
for your attention.
I'm almost proud of my exhaustion
I wear it like a medal
to prove 'she tried'.
But now's the time
to say 'I quit'
and let the pain begin.
Fatigue and pain must fade away
through ticking minutes of my alarm
and only then will I become
more than I was before.

Anon, from Breakdown by Elizabeth Wilde McCormick

Collapsed into the void, a man crawls in circles, his paper eyelids closed over dry red sockets, not knowing that his hands and knees are bleeding.

A state of wellness can be defined as a healthy productive tension which creates movement and produces activity which is kept in momentum by the balance of effort and rest. Exhaustion is the state created when we continually push ourselves beyond ordinary tiredness and fatigue. Exhaustion is maintained and exacerbated when, instead of stopping to appraise our general situation, we press on, disregarding all the physical and psychological signs, and rely on willpower alone to keep us going. Alongside this is the fantasy that by our doing so we will close the gap between what is actually happening and what we wish to happen. Exhaustion is a chronically endured feeling of depletion, weariness, anxiety, boredom, emptiness and general malaise bordering on catabolic imbalance. We may talk about feeling dried out, used up, burnt out, as there is no more juice left, and yet we feel compelled, or doomed, to carry on. We become exhausted when external or internal demands stretch our known responses to the absolute limit. This state may carry on for years, and our world may become smaller and smaller as we seek to try and cope.

On the edge we tend to be unaware of the depth of our own fatigue and exhaustion levels. All our attention is focused on surviving in this narrow place, and we tend to use methods we know best, even if they do not really work. I have seen people who are already giving 16 hours a day to a project who, blinded by fatigue, feel obliged to put in one more hour when their performance begins to drop, rather than take time to restore themselves and put energy into the energy bank. In the image of the spiral we see that our ego–self has extended our effort way beyond itself and far, far away from the influence and nourishment of the self. We feel cut off from the source, prey to our fears and compelled to keep on the weary, repetitive way. We are afraid of stopping because this means facing the edge and the unknown. We fear falling off into a terrible abyss. We fear our emptiness. We fear our internal pain. Or we cannot find a logical reason for feeling so exhausted and begin to add shame to our build-up of inner feelings.

There are also times in all our lives when we just cannot stop. Having to work hard to support a family, to compete in a diminishing job market, to look after elderly parents or difficult teenagers, we are exhausted by the constant emotional demand and there are times in all our lives when we cannot let up. We may also become exhausted by loss and defeat, by striving to give our all only to be met with ingratitude and more demands. So often we carry on, even egged on by defeat, with more determination and effort, as if running from the creature following us or a sense that we are just a hair's breadth away from the chasm opening behind us. And the more we carry on in the old way, compounding our exhaustion, the more desperate we feel, the harder we try, and the more fixed and obsessional we may become in our thinking. We feel like Sisyphus pushing the boulder up the hill. We have a sense of fight in us, fighting to try and gain control or 'get back to normal', but the more we try the less we feel we achieve.

We may remain in this state for two or three years. Then it takes just one apparently small thing, like someone shouting at us in the bank, or the car going wrong, or a neighbour's cat, to trigger our collapse. The breakdown point on the spiral is when we have overextended our effort and willpower to the point of collapse. The collapse heralds our return to the centre again and an opportunity to be in touch with the energy of the self, with time to heal, time to begin to listen to the voice of the self.

Exhaustion can be experienced as follows:

- **Body:** stiff neck and shoulders; tension throughout limbs and in joints; hyperventilation and chest pain; small accidents; sprains, breaks, muscle spasm; menstrual difficulties in women, loss of sexual appetite, or excessive compulsive sexual demand
- **Feelings:** a need to keep in control by repressing feelings; swings of mood from tearfulness to furious rage; feeling empty and afraid; feeling lost
- **Mind:** the *idée fixe*, obsession with getting things done
- **Intuition:** largely blocked but leaking out in swings of superstition and the need for superstitious rituals

Recogizing our state of exhaustion honestly and naming it can be the beginning of relief. After this comes the practical issue of how we address our exhaustion – how do we stop for long enough to let our bodies return to a healthy balance, and how do we cope with the fact of our exhaustion psychologically? Whilst exhaustion is always created by our response to life, and sometimes we do have to live in some very tight corners and edges, learning about our responses to demand always helps us to create a more robust attitude for future demands.

70

CREATIVE BOUNDARIES

We need to create edges between different aspects of our lives so that our time is divided appropriately. As outside, so inside, we need to create boundaries between time for others and time for daily self-renewal. We cannot give out unless we receive in. If we are unable to be still enough or open enough to receive, our well of giving and effort will run dry very quickly.

THE PLACATION TRAP

Some of us find it hard to say no when we need to. This can lead us to taking on inappropriate tasks or spending time with people we really do not like. Why do we do this and where does it come from? People who tend to exhaust themselves often have a poor sense of their real selves, who they really are. They often try and please others as a way of gaining self-esteem or a sense of self. Inside they may feel empty and hollow. Sometimes people say 'I don't feel there is anything inside me.' Work, or other people, then become the main focus, and whilst this works well and esteem is gained, this success is dependent upon constant giving out, effort or activity. The self suffers and has no place, and the person is not in contact with the self. It may pull and tug, in dreams of running to catch a disappearing train, in pains in our necks, in a sickening fall in the stomach, but if these stirrings are banished as shameful or judged as weakness, we do not address them. It then takes something dramatic such as a collapse to bring us round to meeting ourselves. The collapse or breakdown point takes us into darkness and a meeting with unconsciousness. We may remain in this place for a time and need help and support to restore our balance, to learn what it was that brought us here and where we go next.

It may be that the part of us which has been dominant in our lives has actually run out of energy because its time of dominance is up. We do not move in a linear way, we do not use the same parts of ourselves all our lives. Parts of us wax and wane.

James Hillman writes, in *Suicide and the Soul*, 'It is illusory to hope that growth is but an additive process requiring neither sacrifice nor death. The soul favours the death experience to usher in change.' What is it in us that is exhausted and ready to let go? What are we hanging onto that feels so hard to let go of – identity, power, face, skill, external goods, beauty, attachment to substance and control?

Many of us are unaware of the difference between the ego-adapted self and the inner self until we have a crisis. Crisis brings these issues into focus. But we can become aware of our tendency to hurry sickness, to be colour blind to fatigue, to try and run past our own exhaustion. The wife of a cardiac patient who had recently died said to me, 'He behaved as if he could run past death itself.'

KEEPING WELL

Keeping physically well whilst enduring times of hardship and exhaustion is extremely important, as is developing the rituals which will keep us well. It helps to pay special attention to the following, as if you are developing your muscles for a marathon crusade.

- **Sleep.** Make sure you have adequate and restful sleep and note how you feel when you wake. If your sleep is disturbed, if you suffer early morning waking or find it hard to go off to sleep, try first to acknowledge that all is not well and feel into what it is that is preventing you from proper rest. Images are again helpful here. Note the images that surface throughout the night and write them down. What is trying to communicate to you in the dark of night? First we need to hear, and then we need to get some rest. Find a regime that helps you rest, such as physical exercise, abdominal breathing exercises and evening relaxation and visualization. There are many herbal aids to restful sleep available in health shops such as tincture of hops, passiflora and vervein. If your sleep is seriously impaired you may be suffering a clinical depression or physical illness and it is best to take medical advice. If when you have explored all these your sleep is still suffering then let it be and see what comes to you. After meningitis I did not sleep for more than three quarters of an hour for over nine months. After three months, when I felt deranged by fatigue and was cross with my body and impatient with the process, I lay awake in the small twilight hours and received the following communication: 'If something as major as initiation is going on you just cannot sleep on the job.' It made sense and I surrendered to it, and at the same time made sure that about once every ten days I took a small dose of the lethal concoction prescribed by my doctor, which brought me seven blissful hours of unconsciousness.

- **Breathing.** Watch your breathing and make sure you are not hyperventilating. Hyperventilation produces fatigue and feelings of breathlessness, as if you are not getting enough air into your lungs. It can contribute to dizziness, tingling in the hands and feet, lightheadedness and chest pain. Ideally find a good teacher to show you how to do abdominal breathing and practise this three times daily until it comes naturally.
- **Diet.** When we are exhausted we tend to eat on the run and grab easy food, often full of salt and fat, because it carries the illusion of feeding out fatigue. It does not, it only makes things worse. We gain weight and feel heavier, get indigestion and feel bad. Try to bring ritual into your eating; always sit down at a table, sharing the meal with others. Eat healthily and see it as a positive contribution to this time of exhaustion.

EXERCISE: LOOK WITHIN YOURSELF

1 Feel behind your own exhaustion, into your body. How does it speak? What does it say?
2 Name the part of you that has become the driver in your life. What is he/she/it like? Where does this figure come from? How did it get there? What keeps it in charge?
3 Note the difference between the driver self who is hurtling up the spiral trying to gain control, and the self you are leaving behind.
4 What does the self the driver leaves behind wish to say? What does this self need right now? How can you listen to this self and bring it more fully into your life?

5 What purpose does the driver self with its hurry sickness serve? What do you fear might happen if this part were to step back?

6 Ask yourself how you can bear the emptiness you feel in order to allow something new to come in. Think about why you cannot say no. Know how and when to say no.

7 Find the well or source of nourishment by sitting each day, even if for only five minutes, to contemplate this place and imagine yourself drinking from the great eternal wellspring of life's fresh water that will water your parched spirit. However busy, however impoverished our daily life, this image will always be there for us. It is our attitude of accepting its great bounty that we must foster, especially in the midst of our exhaustion. The water of feeling and the water of human kindness can let the parched begin to feel softened; the thirsty can drink, the swollen become healed, the burnt out regenerate, and the flame of exhaustive fear is quelled.

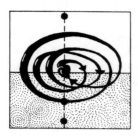

8

Loss and Fear of Loss

Falling, falling, into the dark, into the unknown dark,
hoping to be unbound after the swaddling.
A glimpse of love presses the Chinese feet of hope
that so long ago left me limping badly.
And now, I bargain with hope in the basement of the psyche.

The unvisited ocean swell inside calls me
to unveil my eyes and leap into its vastness.
I fear it is too big for me
so I bargain with my sad trifles,
in small-mindedness:
If I do this, behave well, ask for little
will you send me a kind messenger?
I go over and over what has been, what might have been; if;
  if only;
I keep it small this way and the ocean swells beneath me.

Elizabeth McCormick, 1994

The spiral here becomes like a vortex, pulling us down. We feel
we are falling, down and down, even to death.

A deep sense of loss and being pulled down into it, as if into
death, is part of the darkness of the edge. We feel we are losing,
we are cut off from some central link, from some unnamed vital
source within, and are at risk of spinning into the vortex or abyss.
We feel loss all around us, wondering how we ever felt linked to
anything or anyone of substance. Who are we and where are we
going? We are not in charge. The body feels as if it has lost a
limb, we are hollowed out as if by a blow to the solar plexus; our

hearts are broken, and we yearn for reparation, for restoration; in our guts there lies, like molten lead, a permanent feeling of dread and terror. It is as if we have been abandoned and cut loose by the mighty hand that once held us in its palm, and that now there is no hope for us, we can only fall and keep on falling, descending by both night and day into darkness. And on the way we meet all the other figures who have feared the fall and gone into it.

In Dante's *Inferno* he writes, 'I was so heavy and full of sleep when I first stumbled from the narrow way.' In this lost, stumbling journey through the dark wood Dante finds again consciously his innocence and sense of self. In her commentary on the *Divine Comedy*, Jungian analyst Helen Luke writes:

> There is only one thing that can save a man in such a pass. It is to admit that he is completely lost and just how frightened he is, and to force himself to look up and away for a moment from self-pity and absorption in the ego.

When we begin to look deeply and hear consciously what is happening to us, however frightening, we are developing contact with the transpersonal self which will be our guide throughout the darkness. We do not just plunge into the darkness, but light a small candle to take into the darkened unknown.

UNIVERSAL LOSS

A sense of loss lingers like a trace element in all our life experiences and is a profound aspect of being human. With birth comes loss, as we leave the apparent safety of our private experience with our mother's womb where our life began. Some of us always carry an image of the Paradise Garden where all is green and bountiful and long to return to its bliss and safety, wanting to revisit this image in all our close relationships. Our expectation may result in the warmth of a cosy relationship but it can also lead to our sudden expulsion from the Paradise Garden. Those whose image for the original womb is more linked to the tomb or cage with associated suffocation and entrapment can spend their lives running from any closeness that might claim them back into the dark dungeon.

76

If the passage from birth to adulthood has not been appropriately crossed and there is either the constant regressive pull back to or the hurried flight from the womb, all relationships will press on this place until reparation is made and the crossing borne. Our coming into the place of the edge may well be to do with an event that has again asked us to attend to our attitude. Until we can stand alone and make relationships from a place of individual separateness we are unable to forge the capacity for true togetherness with another. For coming together in the true sense means always accepting difference and separateness. At the edge we are in private relationship with ourselves, with the opportunity to forge a greater mindfulness of the threads within us.

LIFE TRANSITIONS

Other transitions in life that involve both ending and beginning such as going to school, leaving home, getting a first job, moving to university, building our first independent home and family, also carry aspects of loss. We may not notice the loss because we are intent on pressing forward into the new. Any change involves loss of what went before. This is marked according to our previous experience of loss and the feelings already attached to loss. Major losses in early life through death, illness, depression, divorce, constantly moving house or country may remain like unexplored parcels within us, waiting to be opened by the appropriate trigger. Our own stages of life and development also carry many different experiences of loss: loss of childhood innocence, loss of adolescent freedom to experiment, loss of woman- or manhood during menopause, challenges to identity after job loss or change in status, or during social, cultural or financial adjustment. When we are on the edge, our feeling of falling into darkness, losing what we know, particularly of ourselves, is acute. We may have arrived at this place because of actual loss of something important to us – a job, status, money or a loved person or animal – and therefore be in a state of shock and grief for that loss.

LOSS OF SENSE OF SELF

Actual loss may also be the trigger for an awareness of deeper inner loss. It can put us in touch with our fear of losing our central inner attachment. The feeling of loss experienced as being on the edge presents us with a particular deep dread connected with the constant and unfathomable fear, the fear of the loss of self.

The self may call to us, awaken us, by instilling in us this most fearful dread, the dread of losing a self with whom we have never had a proper relationship. Our dread tells us that we must return to connect with the self within us and not to do so is to court psychological death. The self may have called to us; we may have sensed it in our dreams, our waking thoughts and longings, our images and our sense that there is always something else, something beyond the everyday, beyond what we know. But if we do not act upon this call to return consciously to our inner life and forge a link with our self the thread that links ego and self is not strengthened and the axis upon which our life's dance revolves is unstable, even broken. If we have not claimed our real original seed–self and let it show us the way, tuned into its strength, honoured it by listening, we feel like an empty shell. If life is lived only through the ego–personality, which cannot give us the depths and heights, the sense of transcendence, the deeper, wiser self, then we are impoverished and in fear of losing out. An actual external loss may press us on this place, or the threat of our losing our own life through serious illness or accident can awaken in us a terror of dying that comes from our fear of never having truly lived.

What Alice Miller calls the 'provisional life' is the life lived only by the overadapted ego–personality within its severe limitations. In a provisional life we are still living as if it were too dangerous to be our real selves, as if in claiming this self our security from the outside world would shatter, exposing us as the inferior, weak, shameful, unloveable person we fear we are. Many of us build very successful provisional lives in the outside world and shine through our eternal achievements. And for a while these achievements may make us feel good. They work because they help us to emerge into adult life feeling a bit safer. But if this world is built upon the sandy soil of an overadapted or survival self and this is not the whole picture, soon the real seed–self will sound the gong to be heard, and change will be in the air. If we cling on too tightly to the provisional life – and it is hard not to because the fear of returning to childhood pain and ignominy is all too present and frightening, and what we have built may have all the edifices of power, position, money and acceptance – the self will have to rock our sand-built world hard. So through accident, illness, loss, we return both to the original sense of loss of self experienced in childhood and to the opportunity to refind our own innocence and from this build a greater sense of who we really are.

LOSS AS PREPARATION FOR DEATH

People who look at death all the time have a different attitude to life from those who are strangers to death. Life can become more precious because we have known the finality of death. To sit in friendship and laughter with someone who you know has experienced the severest of losses is to be in the presence of someone who has lived the extremes and walked the narrow way between. To be so much in the moment of life is a fantastic gift. To have glimpsed the fact of death, to know the brush of its wings, to have had it take away that which was loved, is to emerge into life and to return to life willing to live every moment with our robust truth and magnificence.

NAMING AND DEFINING THE IMAGE OF OUR LOSS

In accepting the reality of our sense of loss we need to try and locate the different levels of the loss we feel and write them down as external losses and internal losses, naming them fully and all the feelings that accompany them. Sometimes we experience loss as just a black hole. Jeremy Howe, whose wife Lizze was murdered by a student, described in a newspaper interview how he felt his grief over her loss to be like a black hole which was swallowing up his whole life. It was suggested to him that he define the black hole, as small or large, a place he could look into or ring fence. Once we have named our loss and the image we carry for that loss we too are able to choose how to relate to the image in our every day. Some days we will not be able to look at it at all and other days we will rail against its death-defined boundaries. Other times we will return to it with a sense of the observer in us or with our wise transpersonal self and ask for help as to the meaning of this loss in our life. And we must enter a period of grieving for that which has been lost or neglected and begin the task of mourning. The four tasks of mourning are as follows:

- to accept the reality of the loss
- to experience the pain of grief
- to adjust to the environment in which the loved/desired/beloved is missing, which may apply to our hopes, aspirations or beliefs as well as to actual persons
- to withdraw the emotional energy and reinvest it with another relationship – the opportunity, as Jung said, to begin a love affair with one's self, to explore one's own reality, with energy untouched by our response to others for the time being

Loss can make us feel paralysed and sick, misunderstood and bitter, paranoid, suicidal and misunderstood. We may feel betrayed, angry, vengeful. We will feel powerless, victimized, tearful, sick to our stomachs and left pining for what was, for what might have been, our hearts in agonized ache brimming over with the weight and poignancy of our deepest sadness. In *A Grief Observed*, C S Lewis writes:

> No one ever told me grief felt so like fear. I am not afraid, but the sensation is like being afraid. The same fluttering of the stomach, the same restlessness, the yawning. I keep swallowing.

EXERCISE

1 How does your experience of loss make you feel? What are the different feelings you are carrying, what is your image of what you feel? Write about your feelings or paint what you feel.

2 If you feel you are falling, how can you choose to jump, move, swim into the next stage? If we feel we are drowning we can learn to become pearl divers. What climate, geography are you in? What do you need in this place – walking boots, water wings – as you step into the unknown dark, giving up all that has gone before?

3 What are the resolutions you realize you are making about your life? For example, 'I will never try anything again, love again, hope again.' How can you 'be' alongside this hurt part, accepting its hurt? How can you help the hurt part to recover and gain strength so that you might venture forth into life again, however changed?

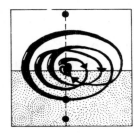

9

Grey Melancholy and Black Depression

Death a relief, release
too easy, beyond reach, beyond will.
Frozen, powerless.
Pray for fear to kill – me? him?
Me, me, me, me
Let me go.
They ask why die?
I scream why live?
No reason
No reason at all.
No God, no person.
no goodness
No comfort, no support.
No relaxation
A yawning abyss of fear to make contact
Why bother?

Marjorie Orr, 'Can I survive?', 1995

The spiral twists and turns in its great spectrum, offering us a map of the patterns reaching from grey melancholy to black depression. Part of the human condition is to feel 'down', sad, blue, low in spirits, melancholic in response to disappointments, loss, difficulty and the awfulness of many of the events going on in the world. To be cast down is appropriate in many circumstances. When we are in the dark and we cannot see, we have to learn to listen, or to move slowly through the dark touching and smelling things, developing our awareness of other ways of being in the world and other functions within ourselves. In our melancholy we have time to be with ourselves, think alone, not have to be pulled into others' needs or be in the limelight. In sadness and melancholy we may take time to visit or be visited by images and the landscape within the unconscious sphere. Melancholy can also be seen as a necessary time of slowing down to aid recovery; it gives us opportunity for healing. And beyond the greys of melancholy to the deepest, darkest places is where we forge links within that can only come from this journey in and through darkness where we remain long enough not to be able to falsify the truth any longer. When the ego cannot rise and take over we forge unforgettable and unfathomable links with the soul. And whereas we would never wish the dark experience of depression consciously on anyone, we may come to realize, after our sentence is passed, that we would not have missed it for the world.

For artists, writers and poets the melancholic state is a necessary place within which to create. The intensity of feeling and the passion needed to survive, name and portray the quality of this place is provided by the half light.

Awareness of the sharpness of the edge when visiting depression and melancholy is highlighted by the development of modern psychiatry and pharmacology. Before the advent of modern psychiatry, psychoanalysis and drugs, in 1876 the great painter Van Gogh was a preacher in England. He wrote in his sermon, 'Our nature is sorrowful. By the sadness of our countenance the heart is made better.' He suffered a lifelong omnipresent though sometimes hidden depression, but his upbringing had taught him to value melancholy. In his psychological biography of the painter, *Stranger on the Earth*, Albert J Lubin writes:

> The story of Vincent Van Gogh is a never-ending struggle to control, modify and glorify or deny a deep-rooted melancholy and loneliness. Religion and art were simply different means he employed for this purpose. He says 'The work helps me avoid that melancholic staring into the abyss.' He made a distinction between what he called 'active melancholy', which was ideal for painting, and a paralyzing depression which leads to despair.

Van Gogh lived on the edge all his life. He moved within a grey melancholic state to the extremes of black depression, almost glorifying suffering, and marginalized himself by his social isolation and shabby dressing, not looking after himself or eating properly. Van Gogh's father told him, 'Sadness does no harm but makes us see things with a holier eye.' The Van Gogh family had high expectations and demands, and several of Vincent's siblings had low self-esteem and emotional problems – one was schizophrenic and two, including Vincent, committed suicide. Vincent describes his image of himself as a young infant as a 'seed exposed to a frosty wind'.

'Treatments' for depression in all its mysterious guises and colours will always be hotly debated. Van Gogh's troubled inner life will be the subject of debate for many years. What if Prozac had been available, or psychoanalysis, perhaps primal scream or transactional analysis? Or what if Vincent had been able to heal his early 'frostbitten' wounds within the transcendence of a loving relationship? What would his paintings have been like? But his story serves to offer us a powerful archetype of suffering and torment in the brilliance of his paintings and that archetypal wound they convey to us speaks to generation after generation and needs no fashion or creed to be identified.

When examining the properties of the edge with our observer approach we need to consider the two polarities posed in this place of depression. The value of grey melancholy on one hand, which is necessary for our wider, deeper communications with our internal landscape, and the paralysing catatonic results of deep, intractable black depression on the other hand. Wisdom serves us when it takes in the wide spectrum of the extremes and seeks to offer a guiding hand throughout. The observing midwifery approach is to watch, support and encourage, to trust the process within even when the path upon which the traveller labours seems to open up or reach a dead end. When emergency looms it would be insane foolishness and misguided hubris not to intervene in order to offer the real meaning of the word asylum. A safe place from the hostile, threatening world experienced in severe depression, where torture and humiliation are omnipresent, becomes the first bridge to healing and stepping out of the black chasm of depression. William Styron, in *Darkness Visible*, writes:

> I'm convinced I should have been in hospital weeks before. Hospital was my salvation. The hospital offered the mild, oddly gratifying

trauma of sudden stabilization – a transfer out of the too familiar surroundings of home, where all is anxiety and discord, into an orderly and benign detention where one's duty is to try to get well. For me the real healers were seclusion and time.

Our spiral map of this place shows that it is of winter in the psyche. The life-force feels on hold, suspended, out of reach. Our world is coloured in greys and muted patterns, nothing stirs, growth is completely hidden, everything feels the same day after day. It may be difficult to know when the process of grey melancholy, necessary for reparation, healing and creation moves into the darker shades of grey and sinister black and our state is more suited to the word 'depression', where we are less in touch with reality, feel possessed only of our internal landscape, enjoy nothing at all, feel ourselves to be on an irrevocable sliding slope to nothingness. At the severe end of his own long depression William Styron writes:

> I had now reached that phase of the disorder where all sense of hope had vanished. My brain had become less an organ of thought than an instrument registering, minute by minute, varying degrees of its own suffering. The mornings themselves were becoming bad now as I wandered about lethargic, following my synthetic sleep, but afternoons were still the worst, beginning at about three o'clock when I'd feel the horror, like some poisonous fogbank, roll in upon my mind, forcing me into bed. There I would lie for as long as six hours, gazing at the ceiling and waiting for that moment of evening when, mysteriously, the crucifixion would ease up just enough to allow me to force down some food and then, like an automaton, seek an hour or two of sleep again.

FORGING A SOUL WITHIN THE VOID

Different people experience depression and melancholy in their own personal way. The hallmarks of black depression are a sense of unrelenting pain and misery with no hope of change. The hopelessness about our situation, that it will never change, weighs heavy on our whole being. It is hard to contact any light or believe in anything good. In this place of deepest darkness, all the lights are shut down. Whatever transpersonal connection we have forged before may feel eclipsed or be hard to hold onto.

85

Often we only have a token awareness that somewhere this light is indeed being held for us by others, by the collective force of transpersonal energy which is the light that ultimately redeems the suffering of the world. At these times, this is all there is, and those holding the light for us in whatever guise hold our soul in their hands. This is the most poignant time, and our experience of travelling within this dark cave of depression when all else is given up may make us feel that we can no longer find any sense of God, whatever God is for us and however strong our beliefs have been previously. This can be the point of utter darkness when we feel forsaken by everything that has gone before, by those who have been with us before and the beliefs we have held before. It is also true that in this place where we cannot find God, we come closer to God than at any other time.

This is the time when our relationship with the God within is forged in the depths of our own soul. The temptation will be to cover up any threat of entering the place of the void with ritual and false beliefs. When we search in organized religion and are told to just pray, or chastized because we do not believe enough, this is also the opportunity to come nearest to naming of the God that lives within us and is for us. The fact of the existence of this transpersonal light is evident from stories of others' travels along this way. Scratched into the walls of one of the basements in a Jewish ghetto in Poland are the words:

> I believe in the sun even when it does not shine;
> I believe in love even when it is not shown;
> I believe in God even when he does not speak.

Evidence comes to me daily of individual struggles to hold onto a glimpse of this light in the darkest of places. What helps people through this place is the fact of others' support and belief in them – in the simple daily reminders, the cards, letters, phone calls that make all the difference. I was once much moved by hearing on a radio programme in the USA of an army colonel responsible for debriefing men serving in Bosnia. He had to sit in his Washington office listening to the stories his men had had to process regarding the massacres of Muslims – men tortured, their wives and daughters raped in front of them before having their throats slit. One day after telling his particular horrific tale, one Muslim soldier had left the army barracks and was later found hanged. Each lunchtime the colonel, in despair over what to do about these horrific stories, would cross the square and visit the Vermeer exhibition, an exhibition which has since claimed the love of the world. And as he sat and gazed at the luminosity of Vermeer's work, which captures the soul in its most tender and exquisite form, he learned that Vermeer too had lived in a time of violent civil unrest in Europe.

Our personal melancholy or depression may be entered through a variety of experiences. Loss which cannot be mourned, anger which cannot be fully expressed, a long-term struggle with the weariness of exhaustion and depletion, frequently results in what we loosely term depression. Depression seems to be an umbrella term used to describe these painful but indeterminate experiences. Many books and articles are written on depression, and many approaches claim 'success'. But we must ask what we hope for out of our encounters with depression. Is it depression into another layer of our being, a going down meaning a deepening, an opportunity to forge a greater robustness for being in life? Depression seems so often the very essence of being human. It is part of humanity's response to an inner or outer world which is terrible that brings us into this place. Not to admit to depression, to try and medicate it away, to manically attempt to run past it or to over-brighten it, would seem to diminish our capacity for the depth of feeling. Statistics show that most people come out of depression, however deeply they have been thrown into it. And many people come out of depression with a greater sense of reverence for the beauty of the world as well as the darkness and misery. It seems to me that reports of depression have increased alongside the growth in demand for excellence – a balancing factor perhaps in a worldview that could become polarized. To be depressed is to be real, and demands that we weigh the balance between what is manageable and what becomes unmanageable.

EXERCISE

1 Where do you feel you are on the spiral between grey melancholy and black depression? Make a chart for yourself showing

the times over the last few months when you have moved between the two. Mark on the chart what times brought you in contact with each and write down something of what was happening then, what you were thinking, doing, involved with, and any images that come to you from that time. Keep this chart for the next few months and let yourself feel in touch with the language and the quality of the rhythm being shown to you.

2 Find an image for grey melancholy. Paint this image and note the language of its geography. Then find an image for your depressed feelings, from the everyday awareness of feeling depressed to the blackest place. Ask that you begin to become aware of what this image refers to and what it most needs from your understanding.

3 Sometimes depression is compounded by negative or depressed thinking about ourselves and our situation. In this way we build what Dorothy Rowe refers to as a 'prison' for ourselves where our thinking confirms a sense of our own worthlessness. Negative thinking can be a trap in that because something has not gone well we presume that other things will not go well and we begin feeding off our gloomy thoughts presuming that our future will be coloured in this way. By recognizing the trap of negative thinking, writing down the specific negative thoughts we catch, we can begin to stand back and ask whether this is true, or whether there is another way we can approach this.

4 If we find that images of depression take us backward in time to some unresolved loss from the past then part of our journey upon the edge is to recognize and meet the pull back to address this loss in whatever way we can. As I said at the beginning, all of us are wounded beings. When the energy still in the original wound calls to us it directs our life-force into that place and we can only enter it and work within it, finding those who will accompany us on that journey to resolve what has previously been unresolvable.

THIS TOO WILL CHANGE

When the natural time has passed and something is resolved then the dawn in our psyche begins to awaken, and the frozen winter begins to thaw. It is time to emerge from darkness and to be awakened. Some people report surprisingly strong volts of feeling beginning to come into their depression – a greater clarity, an actual sense of lightness or divine presence, a greater sense of beauty and connectedness to other people and to the things of nature. One or two people report transcendent and spiritual awakenings where a being with a divine energy shines forth or delivers a message of welcome. These experiences may be in moments only, and there is still the journey to make through the daily routine of depression and melancholy. But the moments of lightness may move us along enough to go gladly, accepting the shroud of depressed awareness, until such time as we are able to emerge fully. And many people report the emergence from the pits of depression as being like a rebirth.

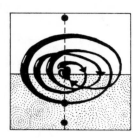

10

Anger and Rage

Heart again – not fear but battered
Like mortar shell
Blows a hole
Chest like bedsprings, punched, a dull thud,
Instant shut down
Again, again, again
Why hope?
Life ebbing away year by year
Elastic hope returns
to teenage cynicism.
Black humour, no laughs now.
Tired, tired. Wasted effort.
A wasted life.
The con worn thin
Who cares?
A few fireflies in the distance
Sporadic, cheering
But too few, too peripheral
Too ungraspable in the yawning abyss

A world of goodness
I cannot reach
Too derelict to try, to think, to hope
for contact.
Too frightened to get what will keep
me alive will kill me.

Marjorie Orr, 'Let Down', 1995

The spiral whirls like a spinning top, blurring all edges; we are spun round, stunned at first, unsure, then twisting in anger; then, lost in the process, caught in the spiralling momentum of rage, beyond ourselves, beside ourselves, out of reach.

Things on the edge feel unfair. Its rigidity and narrow sharpness full of unknowns and fears can make us feel on trial, or tried and found wanting and serving time in punishment, punished for a crime we know not of, but others do. We know we are angry somewhere, but our anger may feel far away, or disconnected from us because it is so hard to pinpoint its actual source. In impotent rage we can feel as if all the world is laughing at us, has seen our folly and judged us an outcast in crime, and will make us suffer.

When something we have held precious seems to be taken away from us for no apparent reason we are naturally outraged, but it can be hard to find expression for what we feel. There is no outward sign of a war, there are no uniformed regiments to join and flags to fly in support of the effort and within which we can fight the enemy. The enemy is within us and we see it everywhere. We feel under constant attack and the extreme end of the spiral brings us persecution and torture. The images flow only too graphically: being on the rack, strung out; held in the stocks; flogged by some sadistic jailor; flayed by the strap; teased and tortured, pressing first our anger, then our rage and then our rage-driven oblivion.

Why me? What have I done? What is it? If only I could know then I could put it right, make amends, get something done. But no one is saying. The world goes on around us, business as usual. Can they not see that we are floundering and seething, that we are deranged prisoners caught in a trap, our appeal pending?

These feelings are more acute if we have reached a time in our life when we feel we had got things about right. We have done all the right things, taken the obvious knocks and medicines, been good, read the right books on personal growth, had therapy, said our prayers, enjoyed modest success and fulfilment, supported others – and then the rug is pulled from under us and the rats start biting. Just as we think we have got it all hung together, everything changes.

At any point in our life the self can begin to sound its drumbeat, calling us to listen to a deeper note and to contact our true purpose. A great tuning fork sounds often at the traditional mid-life point, when the ego–personality is at its peak of development having learned skills and made achievements in the world. We may be tumbled out of a job we believed was secure or a relationship we held dear, or our sense of connection with a belief or life work is seriously challenged. The self is pushing us again and again to keep moving, not to settle for a compromised, unfinished life. We may have thought we were on track and had our path mapped out neatly for the future but the self has something else in mind for us. This is one of those times when we are thrown into anger as an immediate response to being thwarted, but we move into a frame of mind when we hold a deep respect for the self, and learn to be mindful that we, in ego–personality terms, are not in charge. And we may be asked to move along paths we would not consciously have chosen but which are what our life has brought us. Our choice in time is to accept this actual truth in a philosophical way, and to see what we can make of it, or to rail angrily in a passive way, blaming the event or fate or a harsh God or building within ourselves a sense that we are just unlucky. We have an opportunity here to choose not to settle for anything less than excellence.

BILE AND BITTERNESS

But before we can absorb the full meaning of how we might use our anger and rage we must dance in and out of their devastating rhythm by first recognizing the range of feelings surging through us, to allow a raging against the world that has let us down, to kick against the belief we feel has bottomed out, relationships that have not held and most of all the brittle inner fury against ourselves – the awful feeling that we went wrong somewhere, we got it wrong, the going over and over past events, saying 'If I had done this, done that, not done this or that, if I'd been different, if they'd been different'. This kicking out process brings us in touch with sides of ourselves we have never known.

Someone I knew who fell in love for the first time at 50 with a scoundrel who gave her the deepest delights and the deepest sorrow said after the second betrayal, 'Now I know what it feels like to want to stick a knife into someone.' Anger verging on rage is visceral, physical and urgent. It needs equally physical acceptance and expression – *not* sticking a knife into someone, but acting out that blade-thrust into an object that can take the energy and transform it: the earth, water, clay. And to find words and put energy and passion into them, to scream and shout and yell out our rage and bitterness, the greenest bile must be honoured in this grittiest, dirtiest dungeon of rage. Later, when anger is spent, comes the cool shower of relief. Not to honour the feeling of rage is to harden our anger into emotional bitterness and seek literal revenge or to let our bodies take the strain. Anger hardened down into arteries and cells wreaks havoc with our homeostasis. John Hunter, an 18th-century physician wrote: 'My heart is in the hands of any rascal who chooses to annoy me.' He lived out his belief by dropping dead at a medical board meeting after an argument. Perhaps he had not found ways of being angry that were safe. 'My tongue will tell the anger of my heart, or else my heart, concealing it, will break,' says Kate in *The Taming of the Shrew*.

Fran's dream went like this:

> I am standing in deep piles of shit. It is other people's shit as well as mine. Some is old and hard and some is fresh. It is disgusting and frightening. I feel I will never get out of it. Then I look up and there is a shower in the ceiling which begins to sprinkle soft, gentle water onto me. I let the water wash me clean and watch it wash away all the piles of shit.

When we looked at this dream she related the standing in shit to her current job. She had agreed to take on a difficult assignment to please a powerful female boss to whom she was unable to say no. Her boss was herself a very angry woman, often losing her temper, shouting at others, and finding anger in all the corners of her life. Fran had admired this woman because of her energy and hard work and had been happy at first to go along with her plans. She also could see that she hoped some of this woman's forthrightness and fiery energy would rub off on her. Fran had always been afraid of anger, feeling it to be a mark of rejection, so she sought to placate this woman's demands to fend off what felt like an attack, driving any anger she herself had deeper inside her. She became a puppet to this woman's every demand, with her own qualities unvalued and undermined, making her feel put down, a weakling (and like shit) if she did not give in.

The dream graphically shows the layers of 'shittiness' Fran was now up to her ankles in – old shit from the past to do with old angers she had never felt free to express and the new layers from her current situation. She felt that the actual substance of the shit was her own anger she had disowned. She recognized a life of 'swallowing' her own responses, when up against powerful people, and she was being forced to recognize (to stand in) the end result of this swallowing, in the waste and decay of her own repressed feelings. She had taken other people's shit as a matter of course, smiling and pleasing and not minding. The key to change shown by the dream was the looking up. It was when she looked up, away from her need to take shit from other people in order to be liked, and at another dimension, that the scene changed. Looking up can be seen as her self moving her to look beyond her immediate and limiting situation to link with her transpersonal self. At that moment, before the cleansing waters flowed, she was linked to a transpersonal dimension she had found by being willing to stand in, bear and look at the 'shittiness' of her life and the ability of the transpersonal to emerge in such a place and lift us from the dark unseen into the light and joy of seeing. This movement brought the flow of water with its cleansing, healing properties which connected her to a better sense of flow and rhythm. It also showed how easy it was to let go of anger once you decide just to look up!

ANGER DEVELOPMENT

Where does our anger come from – from the ego–personality that wants to kick the world for not recognizing it or going on recognizing it for what it feels it is, or from the self because the life of the self is being thwarted because of the drive and demand of the ego? Or both?

There are many spiral layers to anger. We may naturally have a fiery, angry temperament where we rise up like a flame in response to whatever angers us then die down quickly. We may have grown up in an angry household where the angry response was the most common one, and either joined in and felt comfortable with anger or recoiled from it, avoiding it wherever possible for the rest of our days. Unless we are used to the expression of anger in its positive form – the passions of anger are signals that arouse, fire and initiate, name feelings, trumpet our boundaries, clear the air, get things moving, tell us how much someone cares about something – we might well experience anger in its negative form. For anger never inspires indifference. When we have negative responses to anger we fear it, in ourselves and in others, so we tend to avoid it in others and bury it in ourselves. This means that a head of steam may well build up inside us as it collects all our angry responses down the years that we have repressed and smiled over. Repressed feelings of anger can create polarization within. Rose said:

> I've had huge amounts of anger and I'm just getting to a point where I'm allowed to feel something else. The big problem with anger is you have to let it burn itself out, but with me if I'm not on one extreme then I'm on the other, so if I'm not for then I'm against and I have to be against [powerful figures] because otherwise I'd betray myself. Very dangerous being in the middle . . . then I don't know where I am.

Sometimes our anger inside becomes projected onto others who then have to carry it for us – the government and public transport are often popular targets for this, as are public or media figures who behave in ways that invite our anger as well as confirm our reasons for keeping anger under wraps. As we fear and avoid anger so it can become very split off from us, so that we are not aware of carrying it. There is a common and irritating habit among modern therapists and social workers to insist that people are angry and tell them so even when the person is blissfully unaware and out of touch with any angry feelings. Not until something draws our anger and it enters our bodies can we know it and only then can we claim it and work with it to express the layers of it. It is absolutely no good in the abstract. After hearing someone's life story we may think they should be angry because of the injustices or problems they have suffered, but if the evidence tells us that they are unaware of this dimension in themselves we have to accept it. Sooner or later life will provoke their anger and in the natural course of things we would hope that when this happens they are then ready to manage it rather than be blown away by it. Many of us do not dare to be angry because we have witnessed what terrible things uncontained anger can do. And others have perpetrated upon them such terrible deeds that they are beyond anger and their sense of self is held together not by being angry but by being 'on hold' just in order to survive.

But the place of the edge brings us into our own anger. It is a terror and also a relief. Anger is like a terrifying and tremendous storm that can feel life-threatening and can cause devastation. Some things do get swept away, but after a timely storm which long has been brewing, the air really is cleared and the smell is sweeter than ever before.

CRACKING OUR PERSONAL MIRROR

Many of us survive and mould ourselves on other's acceptance or admiration of us. This means that our sense of ourselves is conditional on others' views and on our keeping those views. We may live for a long time quite happily on these compromised terms, although our relationship with ourselves, with others and with life itself will tend to feel impoverished and limited. But we do not know why. We may be pushed to the edge because of this sense of impoverishment or, if all our identity is caught up in this adaptation, when we lose it we feel devastated. We have been seeking others to mirror back our bright ego–personality and suddenly that mirror is cracked and we are thrown back on our inner sense of impoverishment and become prey to bitterness and rage.

Some of the rage is at the actual event – the person who sacked us or stole our money, or the lover who rejected us. But far, far deeper and more powerful are the energies of a self who was once marginalized by not being seen at all. If we have only ever been loved for the face we show to the world that reflects our parents' or other's glory we become like an object of their command and learn to gain this objectification in our relationships. We dress, slim and preen to be beautiful reflections for others; we work hard and strive to gain admiration which will preen our peacock feathers; we strive for perfection and believe our safety and sense of self is at the end of the rainbow. And we are devastated when it does not work any more. And yet this fall from grace is the very beginning of our real, felt life, when we are truly alive and in the world with all its beauties for their own sake, not having to try, struggle or strive.

In Ovid's myth of Narcissus he describes the long, increasingly desperate search for an appropriate mirror for the self, and the responding 'Echo' from one's own voice. It is possible to transform the rage, envy and bitterness felt at the denial of selfhood that may be exposed after a 'fall from grace'. The pain of this loss of self, often described in psychology as the pathology of narcissim is, to a greater or lesser degree, all part of early human experience and can occur at any time. In *Narcissim and Character Transformation* Nathan Schwatz Salant writes: 'A psychology that recognizes the archetypal power of the Self can also consider the devastating effects of envy, without seeing it simply as a too-negative concept that is consequently of little use.'

We have to put the old worn mirror that we keep showing to others away, stop looking outside for reflection, admiration and feedback to give us a sense of self-worth. We have done that, and it no longer works. Now we have to give birth to our own real self, the self that will bring us answers from inside.

TURNING RAGE AGAINST OURSELVES

Sometimes our anger is so hidden and unconscious and we are so gripped by the misery and unfairness we feel we have suffered that we can only rage against others and ourselves. We cannot see any redeeming features or positive outcomes. And if we drive others away in fatigue – for even the most loyal friends are sorely challenged by breast-beating that goes on for too long – then it's as if we have no one left but ourselves to turn our anger against. This is the time when we are most vulnerable to inviting the suicide within us into the ascendancy. We can recognize this sub-personality by the attitude he, she or it evokes. 'Why bother with this? Who cares anyway? I may as well be dead. No one will miss me. It will be better when I'm gone.'

We may become solely a victim, seeing persecutors every-where, unable to take in goodness. This is the darkest side of this geography, the tightest corner of the spiral. We *must* widen up, we must speak to others of how bad we feel, we must postpone actually harming ourselves. How long can we give ourselves? Another ten minutes whilst we make a phone call? Another day while we make a visit to someone? And if we can recognize how desperate we are then we must give ourselves up to some trusted person to take care of us for a while until this annihilating storm has passed. In Part 3 we will look more deeply into this place.

EXERCISE

Here are some questions we might ask of ourselves in the place of anger.

1 What part of me is angry? What is it like? Find an image and then draw, paint or sculpt. Ask yourself: is this image con-nected to the ego that wants its own way? Is this part con-nected to the ego which wants its own way?
2 Where does this image come from? How long has it been there? How old is the image, what are its characteristics? What does it remind me of?
3 If it is old anger, what needs to happen to it?
4 What purpose does my anger most serve right now?
5 How can I honour the focus my anger holds for me in ways that I can usefully manage?

6 If my anger has never been expressed, what do I need to do to express it, let go of it? Write letters, write a story, dance a furious dance, punch bags, stab the earth?
7 What in me is so angry it wants to die?
8 What in me wants to be born?

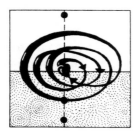

11

Vulnerability

Come into my most sacred place
Loot my abandoned dwelling
I've left myself to make myself acceptable
Coming to your house as your respectful guest
So the shell that is me is vacant and vulnerable
Most of all it is valueless
Because I have left it
I indiscriminately trade myself to make me loveable
Something so easily bartered must come cheap
And is treated so, transgressed against and violated
The issue of prostitution
It is a cruel irony that I give so much for want of love
To find myself horribly lost and without
Dimly I see the panic under which I function
The distance now grown between me and my home –
A sense of belonging
Moves towards reconciliation inspire panic and terror
Messages of compassion anger my suspicion
While my nerves screech with awakening intolerance
As the brutalization of habitual street walking
Can no longer numb the hurt of neglect
Caught between two worlds
A looted building and a fugitive.

Belinda Ackerman, 'The Issue of Prostitution' 1994

On the edge we feel very exposed. So much of our usual way of being has been stripped away from us. We feel as if we know nothing any more and our vulnerability glows like the skin of a hermit crab which has outgrown its shell and needs to find another place to live. Sometimes we feel like Prometheus stranded on a rock with birds pecking at our soft viscera. We feel stuck in our vulnerable place and victim to the elements. We have lost our defences. As Jung writes, an experience of the self is a defeat for the ego. It is as if we have become as a little child, and for the moment are a 'being' vessel without the protection of the original nursery or learned ego shell. We have to endure the pain of not knowing how to be or what to do and imagine that the ground is being prepared for growing, for something new to be born within us. Many of the initiate paths involve being rendered down or actually broken in order to be reborn. Within the chaos of disintegration we must hold onto the image of the gestating fledgling.

CORE WOUNDS

When our core wounds open we feel again as if we were a tiny, fragile young child who was once abandoned, hurt, crushed, teased, humiliated, tortured, damaged. None of our well-learned coping strategies work for us, and we feel stripped bare. As we revisit our core wounding we have the opportunity to use our adult learned consciousness to bring light upon the core, and to bring those feelings and experiences which have been buried into the present time. Core wounds do not go away. What happens is that as we move about the spiral of life experience we meet our wounds differently. In revisiting core wounds we have the opportunity to ask: what needs to be healed? What needs to be strengthened? This job cannot be done whilst we are swinging along in the energy of ego–consciousness in full flight. We have to give up this part of us, or have it given up, so that all our concentration is upon the inner core place. Using the power of the image is helpful. How do we experience our own wounding and what is the nature of that wound? What is our image now of our vulnerable, our most fragile self? Where do we carry it – in our feeling nature, our mind, our bodies? We cannot force, pry, cajole our way through a journey of this kind. We have to be

101

rendered down into it in order to be within it, and our true and authentic answers come from this place. These are times when we need to ask our observer self to be alongside the process, befriending and guiding us when we feel lost for words, helping us through.

Core wounds are invaluable as they keep us human, they remind us that as humans we are vulnerable and fragile. It is in this totally vulnerable place that we have the opportunity to come closer to what is transcendent for us, closer to that divine energy that links us with soul. Our nearness to divine energy, and to the presence of the divine, what we may name God within us, grows through this experience of confrontation with base reality and mortality. The wonder of God cannot grow except through confrontation with human values.

THE NATURE OF THE WOUND

The experience that brings us onto the edge can offer us information about what aspect we may be being asked to strengthen in this barren place. If our core wounding involves difficulty with feeling, and leads us into a crisis in relationships, then perhaps this is what we are being asked to revisit in order to have a different relationship with ourselves and our feeling nature. Many people ask in their loneliness, 'Why does this keep happening to me?' When we examine our patterns, the way we make relationships and the terms on which we make them, we may find, for example, that there is a pattern of choosing people who need us because we need to be needed. It is as if only by being needed do we gain worth. And whilst this may work for a while, if people stop needing us, or we begin to feel taken for granted by others' dependency, we feel exposed and vulnerable again. And we may never have learned to express what it is we really feel or want. So others do not actually know. When we are exposed to our fears, based on the old belief that we are unloveable unless we act, do, give in a certain way determined by others, we can now start asking, 'Does it need to be like this?' And the next step is to begin to release ourselves from the bonds of conditional love in order to take new risks, and to check our newly discovered muscles with a new attitude. We will always be vulnerable to the fear that we are not loveable unless we do what others want, and life may press us on this spot from time to time, but we will be less restricted by the false belief, and as we practise, this old belief will get fainter and fainter.

Falling prey to victim thinking is one of the pitfalls of the vulnerability of the edge. Every time we say, 'He left me' or 'She made me', or 'I was all right until he/she . . .' we are pushing blame onto another and casting in stone our victim mentality. It is awful to abdicate responsibility, it binds us to others in a way that perpetuates our sense of helplessness. Although it is painful to say, 'How can I look at these things that keep happening to me?' or 'What is it in me that keeps attracting these things?', that soon passes as we begin an investigation which can take us beyond our own individual patterns to look at the family we came from, the world family and the realm of archetypal reality.

THE *PUER AETERNUS*

An example of looking archetypally at the struggle within relationships we may be invited into is given by the image offered by the *puer aeternus*, the eternal youth. I use this example because it comes up so often at the place of the edge, particularly in the 'mid-life crisis' and in our search for an integration of our links with heaven and earth. Many men and women carry the theme of the *puer aeternus* in their relationships. They may have a string of short-lived, intense relationships because they are in love with being in love and are afraid of the ground of commitment which makes them feel their wings are being clipped. If they cannot fly, they die. This energy can cause deep heartache all round, for those who are left with a broken heart and for those who carry the wound of fear of suffocation and who can appear heartless. Pushed to the edge, the dance becomes a slow waltz between redeeming the pain of feeling grounded and suffocated, caught in another's web and denied one's spirit, and honouring the magic and exhilaration of the flight – those colourful butterfly wings that can so initiate and charm. The two-way dance is for those who carry this archetypal energy and those who are attracted to its enchantment.

BODY AND MIND EDGES

Our bodies may bring us to the edge and become messengers of new consciousness. The edge may be inviting us to have a new relationship with our sensation function, with the way we use our bodies and the matter and substance around us. It may be a better balancing act that the psyche has in mind. For example, if our core wounding involves the confusion of our feeling and sensation functions, it is the separation of each that allows us to realign. Many of us submerge feeling into our bodies because there is nowhere else for it to go, and we let the body take the strain. We do not do this consciously; we simply swallow our feelings or build body armour around them. It is no coincidence that expressions such as hardhearted, lionhearted and open-hearted refer to the way we present our emotions through our physical presence. Another misappropriation of feeling is to go up into our heads and take on the 'thinker' pose. Many people can identify with the idea of coping by 'rising above things' and living in their heads, inviting the thinking function to think its way through our feelings for us. The expression of feeling or unmanageable states via the vehicle of the body, called somatization, is seen by analyst Joyce MacDougal as an alternative to something nearer to the chaos of madness.

ILLNESS AND ACCIDENT

If we have lived too much, or for long enough, in our heads, in the airiness of the thinking function, our edge may come when we are grounded because of illness or accident. And it is not that we have done anything wrong, it is just that the psyche may be inviting us to readdress the wound to our instinctual, sexual or physical body because the time has come for this. This is not to say that all accident and illness is *because* of a need for balance. Accidents and terrible illnesses happen for reasons we may never know. But how we approach the very real drama of illness and accident makes a difference. For a moment we are the victim again, prey to the fear and helpless rage that this creates, and we may have to go through it first. Then when we are ready, we can move on to be the investigator, the explorer, finding out everything about the intimacy with our physical body–nature our experience has brought us into. When we are ill our body is in the ascendancy and we are invited into the deepest possible relationship and respect for the way it speaks and moves, together with our thoughts and images. We have an opportunity to use this particular edge as a magnificent bridge between inner and outer worlds and watch the interweaving between the two.

There are many mysterious viral illnesses today, with names such as ME, post-viral fatigue syndrome, chronic fatigue syndrome, viral meningitis and encephalitis, as well as allergies to substances, which ground people, myself included, bringing us into what can feel like a twilight world of vulnerability, bringing us into the opportunity of a new relationship with body, instinct and nature. These strange, often undiagnosed, viral illnesses often present similar symptoms to depression, and the search for diagnosis and treatment can move from the biological edge of aleopathic medicine into the complex and mixed edges of the psychiatric and neurological world. As the stories of ME sufferers show, this is always a painful journey. Is it the body, or is it the mind? Am I believed? Is the pain 'true', in as much as we tend to view what is true as needing to show physical evidence. Everyone suffering from any malaise needs to be taken seriously and a plan drawn up for care. It is often only after an exhausting journey through many doctors and potential 'cures', when anger, anxiety and exhaustion have risen, that people move into a pattern of acceptance and begin to receive basic care. Everyone who suffers from physical complaints has a right to the best approaches to their problem that modern medicine has to offer. But the healing process cannot begin to take place until the person's relationship with the physical suffering has been accepted with love. This does not mean resignation or saintly collapse. I see it as a process of active dialogue with an aspect of the body whose cells have either temporarily or permanently changed. This then can become a sub-personality, the part of oneself that perhaps we know least well – or perhaps all too well – which is 'diseased', poorly functioning, stubborn, sad, worn out, or an active multifaceted cellular organism. This means that we are in communication with our illness or physically damaged part, however disturbing this may be. In *A Leg to Stand On* the famous neurologist Oliver Sachs writes with exquisite clarity about his experiences following a severe accident to the musculature and ligaments of his leg. He 'lost' his leg in terms of both his physical location of it and the internal image he carried of it. Deeply disturbed by this breakdown of sensation and feeling, and after his leg had assumed an eerier character, he writes:

> In this limbo, when I journeyed to despair and back – a journey of the soul – I could not turn to science. Faced with a reality which reason could not solve, I turned to art and religion for comfort. It was these, and only these, that could call through the night.

There are many current studies from psychoneuroimmunology and from the alternative approaches to medicine which research the relationship between personality, energy flow, consciousness shifts, life changes and their effects on the body. Eastern approaches to the body work with the whole person, and with the central images of the nervous system and the immune system as being central to one's wellbeing. When we address the core, it seems, by whatever metaphor, inner or outer, we move into a different relationship with ourselves as a whole, and perhaps true healing begins at this interface or bridge.

DEPENDENCY

When we have to take time off from work or from commitments in order to look after our most vulnerable needs or to be looked after and receive the care of others, we are at our most vulnerable. It may be the first time we have had to receive from others in such a way and we may be terrified of being dependent. Many core fears arise with the threat or actuality of dependency. If we have fought hard for control, it is hard for us to be a patient, to have to exercise patience, and to be like a small child, without power or trappings of any kind. We will inevitably go through a whole spiral of difficult feelings related to this experience. At the same time a part of us will be hugely relieved. To have to carry on working and giving to others, meeting deadlines when one is feeling ill and fragile is a terrible conflict. Many of us fight on to the desperate end because we so fear giving in to vulnerability. We fear being picked off like jungle animals by those who are stronger and covet our place. But to use the time, and often we need a great deal of time in order to come into and meet this place properly and be quite rendered down, can be so immensely valuable that we can emerge more grateful for the experience than we could ever have imagined. Only by accepting the reality of our dependence can we become truly independent.

Time, and within that time the dance between one's attitude to ego and to self, seem the crucial ingredients. When we are grounded in this way we are slowed right down. Often we cannot move much or think clearly. Reason and physical action are suspended. We are in the world of feelings and intuition, we can only listen to the voices inside and wait for the threads to come together.

WHO HAS THE BODY?

Sometimes it is helpful to imagine which part of us, which sub-personality, has the body at any one time. When we are feeling particularly fragile, or in pain, or confused, it can help to ask: who are you in there? And to allow an image for this personality, its colour, shape, size, quality. Paint or draw the image, name it, speak with it, ask it about itself. Get to know it as it keeps appearing in your struggle. Befriend it and allow it to have a life within you. Some people discover caged birds, prisoners in a cell, fugitives, bonsai trees, dwarfs and Gypsies who have been without position or words, living within us, only able to use the body as a form of communication. The following poem came out of my own experience with meningitis.

> My body knows something before I do.
> In its tightness, its hurt
> the way it shuts down
> it is saying something
> that I cannot.

107

The inner artist paints the wound
on body's blank canvas.
Tunnel headache, black and blind
ears thundering bells of doom
nerves stretched on the rack of life
the purple red of a bursting heart.

Body becomes the last refuge for
what has lost the right to speak
the rejected and the unborn
a prison dustbin.

Early on in life, who gives us words for feelings?
'I'm scared.'
'I'm cross.'
'I'm lost.'
'I think my little sister will take my place.'
'I want Uncle Arthur to die.'

Body and feelings are civilized early
tailored to fit.
Bound with expectations as a prisoner is bound with
   prison bars.
Don't feel
Just get on with it.
Don't stop
until you achieve something.
Don't weep
pull yourself together.
You'll get over it.
You're no different from a thousand others.

Body becomes prison and prison guard
over imprisoned feelings
swallowing over them
hardening them down
diverting appetites
and the soul quietly starves in the darkness.

Vulnerability

Until the day of liberation
until the body refuses to be the mediator
without a union card
and the colours of the prison dustbin cover the canvas.
Feelings now run through body's bars
in a language that will not lie
or lie down
smoulder, stab, ache, burn, cut, steam, boil, creep, pull,
    snag, fester
to unfold a story. My story, that WILL be told.

ASYLUM

Sometimes we feel so vulnerable we have to take time out to protect ourselves. Sometimes we need to be free of the daily demand and grind in order to let scar tissue form over our vulnerable wounds, and for our open state to be taken care of.

It is always difficult to find places of real asylum, where we are allowed just to be vulnerable for a while and not expected to do much. Psychiatric hospitals seem to take on this role for most people, just as convalescent homes tend to be for those recovering from an identified physical difficulty. It would be ideal to have places where we could go to recover from the burnout of life, to spend unstructured time and be basically cared for at minimal expense or fuss, but sadly these places are rare. The expensive health farm or spa is available only to the few, and even then their programmes can be active and over-positive. But once we have realized what it is we need, asylum can be offered through friends and family, by the familiar, by a caring community, until such time as we find our feet again.

POSITIVE ASPECTS OF VULNERABILITY

1 It is an opportunity for acknowledging, knowing and healing an aspect of core pain to make way for its transformation.
2 True humility can be gained only through the acceptance of vulnerability.

3 We have the opportunity to receive care and kindness from others and they to give it to us. If this is a new experience it is profound. We never forget our humanity after this.
4 After being rendered down we may be reborn.
5 It provides an opportunity to come closer to the divine energy within us.

PITFALLS AND DANGERS

1 In our vulnerability we are open both to positive support and energy coming in and to false prophets and those who seek to 'save' us. We need our guides and other trusted people to hold a positive thread that is right for us, whilst we find our way.
2 Too much exposure can cause weariness and the temptation to give up.
3 If we are too raw, we bleed too heavily, and we need a 'wise midwife' who knows when to call in appropriate help.
4 The desire to blot out pain with medication is strong. Some medication support such as mild tranquillizers are a help only in moderation and only for crisis times.
5 The search for 'cure' and literalization of pain can be strong but can lead us on a wild goose chase, only adding to our burden – see Part 3.

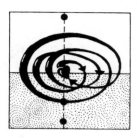

12
Aloneness and Alienation

The smallest fragment can open a door
inside the heart.
Even in the midst of bleakness,
lonely and alone
when time is not a friend
and the grey dawn only blackens
there can be
this
bliss.

Elizabeth McCormick, 'The Pearl of Great Price' 1994

Once again the spiral twists wide. There is a gap. It feels like a point of no return, when we are most extended, when we feel alone in our bleakness, when we can feel as if we are alone in all the world, the last person left.

We make this journey on the edge alone. Whilst we may well be guided by the footsteps and whispers of others who have trodden this way, no one can do it for us. We are ultimately alone within the privacy of our personality and the music of our soul. And it is precisely this journey alone that forges the inner dialogue we need to have with the self who is emerging, the self we realize is now in ascendancy within us. Many people say to me, 'Oh why do I have to do everything on my own?', meaning 'Who will hold my hand, tell me what to do?' We can hide and escape and imagine that things are better in a crowd. We can be seduced by activity or by losing ourselves in relationships. But aloneness is vital here because we really do need to clear the space to hear what is really going on.

THE INTIMACY OF ALONENESS

We need to learn about real intimacy and how to nurture and guard our intimate space so that it becomes the inner treasure from which all things grow, from which stems the true spiritual life and into which others come by invitation only. If we are repeatedly pulled to respond to another person's agenda, another's voice or demand, we can become drained of energy and feel mindless and empty, and our loneliness is accentuated. If we have to try constantly to separate ourselves from the chatter of the crowd, we will not hear our emerging self. And we are the only ones who must hear; if we do not, then no one else will.

Many people cannot bear the burden of aloneness. It puts them too immediately in touch with their core pain, the pain they have covered up by coping strategies. Our Western society today has developed formidable structures for shutting out silence, perhaps in the mistaken assumption that noise helps us to feel less alone. And whereas people who are lonely gain great comfort from talk shows and phone-ins, especially in the small dark hours, the persistent demand to be social and have a jolly time and the noise of television, radio and newspapers can prevent us from hearing the music inside us.

One of the hallmarks of the therapeutic encounter is that it gives people permission to think quietly about themselves and to develop an intimacy with the inner life. A sense of trust that there is more inside than we ever dreamed of, that we all have within us the resources we need to love, cherish and grow happy and wise in moments is one of the great gifts that can be offered by psychotherapy.

Being free to be alone does become more difficult as life itself becomes fuller and busier with causes, campaigns, opinions, tasks – our world is full of clutter and objects. But there are also trees and gardens, oceans, rivers, woods and fields by which we might rest and from which great beauty is offered to us. We are not encouraged to be alone, and the term 'loner' today has painful and dangerous connotations. We are encouraged to be social beings, in relationships with others, and it is often judged as the hallmark of success in life to have had happy and consistent relationships. Yet our relationship with ourselves is the very basis from which all other relationships grow. If we are comfortable with being alone and can become resourceful in this place we make relationships on a freer basis than if we need others to fill our emptiness. True solitude offers contemplation from which we may become refreshed and grow wise.

LOVE

Our capacity for love and intimacy grows early on with our first experience of love and the nature of that love. Being loved just for oneself is the greatest gift one person can bestow on another. But many people forge a capacity to love despite never having been shown love. This is for me one of the wonders of the world. And, in my experience, it is never too late to learn to give love and later, for it is more difficult, to receive love. By just deciding to, we can choose to be more loving. It is never too late to have a happy childhood. The more we practise love the more love we have to offer and are offered in return, and the more love there is to go around. All human beings long for love and thrive on it. When it is truly born from an authentic place it is not sentimental or misguided soft love but the most powerful redeeming connection humans ever make.

THE PAIN OF ALIENATION

When aloneness is most severe in its negative form it can feel like a state of alienation. We feel separate from others, from our social group, from any group, from the world. We feel separate from anything of meaning, alienated from within ourselves, strangers to ourselves, cast off, cut off, an alien on the planet. The Man Who Fell to Earth goes looking for ways to get home to where he came from. In *ET*, the extra terrestrial nearly dies because he is uprooted from where he belongs. Many of us feel like ET and we want to 'go home'.

113

What is 'going home' for us as mortals? Where is home? How do we imagine it for ourselves? Where do we need to really belong, and who is to be our family? Within the body of mankind, who are our soul brothers and sisters, mothers and fathers, relatives, who are the kindred spirits who have made their way via similar routes to ours, within whom we find succour and warmth in times of dire need, who offer us a guiding hand, a smile, a kindness? In our place of alienation we are extremely aware of who is with us along the way, who sees us, like the woman at the well who offered Jesus water when he was on his way to the cross, abandoned and forsaken, alienated from his life's effort. Who dares touch us like Damien of Molokai, when we feel like a leper and are abandoned to the elements? Who comes searching for us when we are lost as Virgil came to Dante in his dark wood? Who might be our avenging angel? Who notices our alienation in the midst of the crowd and gives us the smile of welcome, the soul smile on the figures in Michelangelo's *Pieta*? Who, or what, when we look back upon dark woods or passages, has been there for us all the time?

Accept aloneness for this part of your journey in life and choose solitude. Be aware of the voice that moves you from chosen solitude into alienation. Note images from this place and check what they mean.

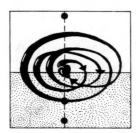

13

Meeting the Trickster

The star it winked at me
lightening the wings of a heavy heart.
I blessed the wink and took it in
and a glittering diamond found
that shone brightly,
that made poetry and dancing.
When the light darkened and the dance faded
mockery threatened.
In terror of loss I sought to press harder as
the tinsel glass pressed upon me.
Madness.
Then awake to the hunger that must seek its own truth.

Elizabeth McCormick, 'The Trickster had Blue Eyes', 1994

The energy of the trickster tends to bring a demonic note into our lives and is very much present when we are on the edge. It is as if we are having to contemplate two worlds, the 'real' world of everyday reality that we have known and the underworld of peculiar irrational episodes and delight. In earlier cultures tricksters were known as the 'delight makers' because they contained the pure instinctual energy which was present before consciousness reached the level where it could observe and objectify what it saw. Tricksters have a dual nature, half animal, half divine, and are able to change themselves into other forms, play magic pranks, and used to appear in carnival culture, in the court jester and the fool, and in folklore as Tom Thumb, Stupid Hans. They appear stupid because of their state of pre-consciousness, but they also possess tremendous powers of healing and transformation. If trickster energy is continually repressed or literalized it can take on a more extreme demonic nature that we would call the Devil. In the Golden Age, figures carrying this energy were seen as the forerunners of the saviour. They were God, man and animal all at once, subhuman and superhuman and unconscious.

It is through this level of deep unconsciousness that trickster energy communicates to us. Tricksters can turn themselves into anything and make things move about. Trickster energy is behind many of the things that go wrong for which we have no rational explanation. This energy may be present in the outside – the fairies that come in the night and steal the milk, the dwarfs who dance on the table leaving their boot marks, crop cycles, UFO sightings, hoaxes – and it may be behind the slips of the tongue, the pranks, the things we do 'for the hell of it' and the dangerous liaisons that we allow ourselves to be drawn into. This energy is like its name – tricky and incredibly exciting, compelling, and also dangerous and demonic, even leading us toward 'hell'. Once again it is our relationship with the energy that makes the difference as to its potentially destructive aspect.

Trickster figures may be obvious, like the magician or sorcerer or those figures in our dreams which are half man, half beast, like the Minotaur, who offer us the combination of human and animal energy, things that combine the human rational world and the deeply primitive instinctual world of beasts but which are also magical and can turn themselves about. We do not understand them and we may feel repelled, but we are drawn into them. They get under our skin. We fall easily under their spell, especially if we have been over-conscious, too much in ego–consciousness for too long. The alchemical figure Mercurius and the mythological god Hermes come into play when we take ourselves too seriously, or are puffed up or too literal, or when we have not attended to something as deeply as we should have. When we are about to give a paper at a grand conference and one of the papers goes missing, or we have a date with someone we want to impress for egoistical reasons and we ladder a stocking or forget to sew on a button, the tricksters show us up, lay us bare, render us ridiculous for the purpose of naming our pride, our cheating and our laziness.

In everyday life, and much more hidden, are the ordinary

people we meet who carry the trickster energy, people who prick balloons, who say the unsayable, who seem immoral, those who charm and seduce us, those into whose arms we would fling ourselves in rapture in order to be transported to another, better, world. It is the trickster voice which says, 'It doesn't matter' when we feel we should obey the rules, and leads us off elsewhere to play truant; who says 'Just one more drink' when we know we have had enough and to court more is to invite in the addict in us. The trickster has no sense of time or morality and is not interested in relating. Trickster energy is behind that compulsion for just one more bite of the cherry. And on an unconscious level it is the trickster who is behind all kinds of scrapes, awkward situations and mistakes in which we find ourselves, not knowing how we got there. Trickster energy invites us into a dangerous love affair – with the bottle, with drugs, with sex, money, gambling, power. Trickster energy will tease us into the apparent charms of these tasty morsels and carry us far on their ocean wave, and we will have a wonderful time – for a while.

As humans we have to meet the trickster energy, recognize it for what it is and forge a relationship with what is right for us. We must find a way in our humanness to resist the temptations of the trickster in order to return, saddened perhaps but wiser and having had a good prank, to our quest as humans. We will have had an adventure and it will be worth while but not if we linger too long. The trickster will play with us until we learn to separate what the trickster energy brings us in the way of initiation and heralding the new and what is merely gross and repetitive. For the trickster is primitive and the intention is to awaken us. It will not change and for all our longing, wanting, pleading or protesting we cannot make the trickster change. But we can let the trickster energy change our relationship with both creative and primitive and instinctual energy.

AWAKENING

Trickster energy awakens in us something that has been dormant or repressed or unlived. It plunges us into areas we would never choose. It pulls us into the opposite. It tears off any masks we might have been wearing. It leads to the fall from grace of high-profile people, the puncturing of the pompous, the challenging of the over-secure, the over-literal, the over-confident. And some people seem to carry more trickster energy than others and live within the trickster mode; they are identified with it as if their life mission were to bring in change for the collective. They are often the least popular, the scapegoats, the people prepared to receive and carry the shadow. In Christian imagery it is Judas who carries trickster energy which takes over and allows one of the most meaningful stories to be revealed to us for 2,000 years.

Tricksters are dangerous, exploitative, unrelated, and if their energy is repressed it can be murderous on the scale of Antichrist figures such as Adolf Hitler. This is why earlier cultures always had the carnival figures, the official jesters and fool figures who drew out and were prepared to carry our mockery, instinctual and primitive connections for the half human, half animal, who could make these energies conscious and keep them in the realm of play and merriment, and keep omnipotent power in its place. *The Rocky Horror Show* was recently unexpectedly popular perhaps for just these reasons. If we can truly carry this edge within ourselves and within our culture, we come nearer to the potential the trickster carries for initiation into a wider, wiser self and to accepting its role in bringing transformation.

It is when we are up against trickster energy that we forge our human capacity to be separate, with a truly definitive and discerning consciousness, and that we begin to come nearest to the Divine. Tricksters remind us that we need to see things with fresh eyes. In *Daimonic Reality*, Patrick Harpur writes:

> Hermes Mercurius does not unmask. He needs no satisfaction from the look on our faces. He forces us to unmask ourselves in the face of his emissaries – enigmatic marks on cornfields, big-eyed aliens who abduct us into spacecraft, 'frustrators' who dictate gibberish through automatic writing, entities whose revelations are delusions and whose delusions, if we persist in them, can lead to revelation. He manipulates us, knows our every thought – knows us better than we know ourselves. He is secretive, ruthless, impersonal and inhuman. Like a psychopath. Like a god. He is less the Devil than Lucifer, who deceives both in order to destroy and in order to bring light. If we do not know ourselves – that is, know, discern, heed our daimons and demons – we are easy meat.

118

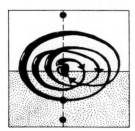

14

Waiting

I said to my soul, be still, and wait without hope
For hope would be hope of the wrong thing; wait without
   love
For love would be love of the wrong thing; there is yet faith
But the faith and the love and the hope are all in the waiting.

T S Eliot, 'East Coker Part III',
from *Collected Poems 1909–1926*

When we have been living on the edge for a long time we may feel as if we will be waiting for ever for something to change. It is the fact of our waiting that brings us into ourselves most deeply. The other properties of the edge all describe action – how we might relate to, think about and respond to the geography and climate of the particular place. But waiting is over all, it is the common ingredient throughout this journey. It is the one extraordinary factor which, in itself, by itself, is the container for the forging process. Like cooking and alchemy we place the ingredients which we have chosen, sorted, handled and thus related to, into a place where time and certain temperatures do the rest. As we are learning now with research experiments, the relationship of the researcher to his or her research is the hidden ingredient that affects the outcome. As Ken Wilbur writes, the thumb prints of the mapmaker are always on the map. Our own experience of waiting is the process of forging our own change within ourselves. And, like the process of gestation in preparation for birth, it takes the time it takes. Too quick and we get abortion, too early and we get a premature, sickly, struggling infant, too late and we are overboiled, overcooked. Change does not come quickly on the deep, psephological level, that complete and utter acceptance of life's process when we know most truly that we cannot push the river, that our task is to let it show us the nature of its flow at this current time, to go with this watery pace and let it find its own level. There may be small changes and adjustments going on all the time and we are best able to witness them when our journey moves us away from the edge enough for us to see.

There is a difference between active waiting and passive collapse and resigned giving up. Active waiting involves us in a relationship with ourselves and our everyday. It means removing any expectations or demands of the time, it means truly living in the moment. This sounds easy but it is often very difficult. We must resist our desire for instant gratification. Nothing on the edge is sorted out in an instant.

A PLACE TO WAIT IN

Part of the great challenge of the edge is that the place is so narrow and frequently dark that often all we can do is wait it out. With the image for the edge that we found at the beginning it is helpful to find another image for the place we might wait out our time or voyage throughout the edge. It may be imagining a safe nest, building a straw fence around us or a tent or rondavel, and putting ourselves there imaginatively several times each day, every day going back to this place, where we just wait. If there is water on our edge we may find the image of a small boat, a canoe or a log. We may furnish each image for our safe space within which to journey with utensils, mandalas, special linings.

FEMININE PRINCIPLE

Waiting invites us to have a new relationship with the dark, with the *yin* or feminine principle, with the unknown. It is only when we have to wait that we begin to see things we would not normally look at. Waiting under a tree we see the movements of the leaves, the patterns of the bark, the fruits that we have taken for granted. Animals and insects scurrying about, who need the tree for their livelihoods, become known to us – the beady-eyed grey squirrel carrying an acorn or peeling back a beechnut, the ants about a fallen leaf, the green woodpecker with his red hat and piercing call. Waiting at an Underground station we see the vast array of human beings in varying bodies and dress, all in their own private worlds with their own private story, making a journey to somewhere.

We will have to go through the initial chaotic period, when waiting just feels like mindless nothing and we want to scream and yell and rush into something new or fill our time by busyness, any busyness. Then our times may be filled with the grey melancholy of depression, the loneliness of being alone, of not being able to communicate.

Waiting in our aloneness we begin to hear the rhythm of our own heartbeat, the flow of our own blood, the pattern of our thoughts, the whisper of the unbidden new and the unthought known. We begin to sense that something lives in us that is not of our own doing. That there really is something in and beyond our previous awareness that transcends our everyday, and if it is in the process of being born to us its passage is as vital and unstoppable as any other natural birth. Our acceptance, our welcome even, when we have not asked to be pregnant means that we meet the new and unexpected with our innocence and truth. This moment is captured with great reverence in several of the great paintings of the Annunciation of Mary, where she sits alone waiting, in contemplation, usually doing some simple task, and she looks up and with a look of rapture on her face receives the Holy Spirit.

ACUTE AWARENESS

The edge demands our most acute awareness. We pay attention to every detail that befalls us. The limitation of ego–control helps us in this process as we can only put one foot in front of the other, or just record what is happening to us on the most minute level. This means paying attention to our dreams, our thoughts, our body sensations, our feelings, to people who contact us, what we see in the outside world, the happenings within our immediate world. In this way we forge a new relationship with our unconscious world, we allow pathways to develop that help us communicate to and from this place. It is easy to fall into the habit of avoiding the acute awareness in waiting. It is very easy to fall into avoiding the true depth experience potential of waiting by filling the gap. Often people say 'I'm bored', 'depressed', 'restless'; or they rush about filling time with busyness for its own sake. When we recognize that it is necessary for us to experience active waiting we have to learn just to 'be'. We need to ask ourselves, before we take any action: 'What purpose does this serve?'

EXERCISE

1 Practise using your image for waiting and the vessel that is to be your container – its feel, its quality, its usefulness to you.

2 Practise active waiting by keeping a journal to write down dreams, thoughts, feelings, sayings, quotations, titles of books, questions you find circulating around you – anything of note that touches you. Use the mandala or lotus image to keep in touch with the energy of the self.

3 Be mindful of filling your waiting time with too much action, whether it is phone calls, food, alcohol, inappropriate medication or people. If you feel the urge to do this pay attention to the aspect of the waiting that feels most unbearable. Know it and be in it and, if you cannot bear it, know that your busyness is in response to what you find unbearable. This knowledge means that you take up whatever busyness you need in a conscious way rather than in a passive, avoiding way. And forgive yourself!

4 Know that the time of waiting in the form you find most excruciating will pass, that given the opportunity of gestation and creative outcome, there is always a passage from terrible waiting through the threshold into the next phase, the dawn or birth of something real that emerges only after the waiting has served its time.

Part Three

DANGERS OF THE EDGE

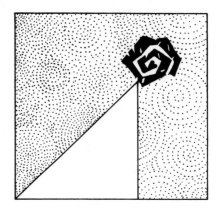

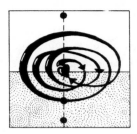

15

What Are the Dangers?

In each of the nine properties of the edge we have looked at the positive and negative aspects particular to each. We have seen that the journey on the edge will always hold the potential of living danger, which is a part of being alive. This dangerous aspect is also something that can attract or repel, determining our response to life decisions. Falling off the edge or being sucked into the vortex is always a possibility, and it is a fear humans carry universally.

This section looks specifically at the main dangers that can occur when energy is diverted from the tasks of each property as a quest, and misplaced by the ego–self. I see this misplacement as something that occurs when we think and act literally and with tunnel vision, without allowing the dance between the language of ego–self axis to take place, when we do not allow what is happening to be held in the wise cloth of the sentient heart and hear the beat of that heart, when we are at risk of falling into extremes, into one of the opposites that our edge is trying to hold. If we confuse waiting and not knowing with boredom, for example, we may rush headlong into any activity just to relieve ourselves of this feeling. Because the journey on the edge is daunting, we may fall at the first gate and decide to give up, living automatically or in denial of an inner life that calls us. We may fall at any gate at any time and our falling may result in disablement or resurrection or both. It seems as if we are at our most vulnerable when the journey of the edge stays in one place for too long and our endurance becomes sorely tested. We want a short cut or a quick-fix solution. As we have seen so far, there are no quick-fix solutions to this path which has many tests of the ego–self axis along the way. But our longing for change may assert itself in our preoccupation with solutions and the seduction these solutions carry. The solutions to a way out of our predicament tend to come in the form of false gods who we believe will bale us out and take our burden from us; or in courting death through suicide.

FALSE GODS AND PROPHETS, AND ADDICTION

Many people and ideas can form themselves as false gods, god-desses and prophets inside us. The voice of the false god or prophet declares with utmost authority: 'This will save you', or 'I've got just what you need', or 'Come with me and be my love.' The offering of the false god may appear in the form of alcohol, drugs, sex, love, money, power for its own sake, New Age cultism or guru religion. The common denominator of the false gods is the powerful seduction and promise to get 'high' and come off the fragility of the edge, to rest one's weary head on the breast or pillow of this wonderful 'other' and be transported, as if by magic, into a never-never land where we do not have to grow up and everything bad is someone else's fault. We want the responsibility for being human and the acute loneliness this often reveals removed from us. We want someone else to tell us what to do, to dictate our daily grind and ritual, to relieve the weight of the momentous journey of soul-forging.

The immediate gain is often a clue to the falseness of the god we feel we have found. We may feel 'high', transported far beyond what we ever imagined possible, and think that at last this is *it*, we have found God. We may look back and despise where we have come from, we may reject all that has gone before, trying to discard our old struggling self as a pathetic creature who is only fit for the bin. But our 'solution' tends not to lead us into wider fields but into the narrow and desperate path of addiction, where all energy goes to serve the addiction god itself. The understanding we need in this place is profound, to acknowledge the extent of our fear and terror and our longing for a solution. The downside is a crash. When gods are false their promise is hollow and only too quickly we are thrown back on our dependency and addiction, and all the pitfalls they bring. Worst of all is the realization that our edges are still there. Whatever the promise of the false gods to relieve us of suffering or indecision, we return to face these inner issues when the path we ventured upon turns into a blind alley. And added to the burden of the edge we now have the chemical burden of addiction, whether it is the adrenalin rush of simulated worship offered in cults or in the taste of power, or the nicotine, cocaine, crack or alcohol rush. Following the false gods may take us on a wide detour, and it may be necessary in some way to bring us to a vital point. In her book *Witness to the Fire*, Linda Schierse Leonard writes:

> The turning point for my addiction was at the bottom of an unfathomable abyss – in a detox ward. There I faced my death, and I also clearly heard the call to life. After years of trying to stop myself drinking I felt helpless and humiliated. At that moment, on my knees in prayer, I admitted I was powerless.

She writes movingly about the miracle of being with others also brought to their knees by addiction, who make a pledge to commit themselves to return to life.

> I learned that this required daily commitment, a vow to life each day, and that the ultimate issue was not merely to stop the physical act of drinking but to face the very meaning of my life – not conditionally as I had done before, but with my very blood.

The promise of the false gods may feel like nectar to the thirsty but the delivery is short-lived and its promise hollow. Addiction brings us to other edges. But it may yet be the place we have to come to to find ourselves at rock bottom.

DESPERATE DECISIONS

All of us can look back on our lives and see decisions taken out of desperation and in ignorance of any alternative. We may live to feel sad, even regret decisions we made – in partnerships, jobs, travel, health – that have ramifications for the rest of our lives. There is no such thing as perfection. We all have to live with these threads of desperation and try and not think of them as mistakes, but as something we chose which was based upon the limitation of our awareness then. But we do not need to do the same things twice from the same place of desperation. Once we are able to reflect, and have become conscious of our ways, our paths, our tendencies, we do have wider choices, even if the only alternative to a hasty decision is just more waiting. What seems important to watch out for is that we do not allow the extremes of the feelings at the edge to push us into further desperate decisions simply because we want a quick-fix solution, or because we have not yet practised endurance for long enough. The question we need to be addressing is: what is the nature of the feeling behind the urge to make a quick decision?

Consider the plight of a woman whose youngest child has just started school. She returns to work but work has changed and her attachment to it has changed. She feels scared and is unsure what to do. She could go to college and retrain, and she looks listlessly through the brochures, but nothing grabs her. She has never wanted a 'career' and is not interested in voluntary work. Staying on at the shop work she is used to is comfortable but not much fun. She is listless and bored. She starts hanging round the school playground with other waiting mothers, some of whom have prams and pushchairs. She begins to look in the prams. She may actively decide to become pregnant again, or she just may 'forget' to use contraception. Either way, her decision is made, and her next five years are taken care of. This may turn out to be a wonderful addition to the family which is never regretted, but the chances are that the listlessness and boredom will return at some point, perhaps at about the time the children are about to leave home. The time of attending to those feelings will only have been postponed. If it is a happy and welcome postponement then it is of no concern, but if the initial feelings have festered and boiled over it may be harder to address them properly. This same process can occur when we make desperate decisions out of a refusal to be fully conscious and present as to our state of mind and our reasons for action. We can see this in people who drift into marriage to get away from home or other unsatisfactory situations; who accept a job in another country to avoid making a decision about emotional commitment; who take a huge pay rise rather than stand up for their viewpoint – to be bought off and rendered impotent can be a desperate decision we repent at leisure.

DRUGS AND OPERATIONS

Sometimes a way to get off the edge if it is manifested through our bodies is to undergo a plan of tests and investigations. I have written elsewhere about the way in which psychic pain can be carried via the body and express itself in physical symptoms. When this is looked at only literally and drugs are offered or operations performed, the source of the pain is not located but simply transferred to another part of the body or another time. Examples of this can be seen in the spinal fusions and hysterectomies that are performed to relieve the symptoms which in fact persist afterwards. If, before any physical investigation, we were able to spend time with our bodies and minds asking for an image, for questions as to the nature of our deep feelings, we might have a lot of surprises! The operations may well need to go ahead, but on a very different basis than if we just enter into these serious situations automatically and with a closed mind, making it a desperate decision. We know, for example, that many presenting symptoms such as heavy bleeding for which hysterectomies are performed, chest pain for which invasive tests are performed and sometimes bypass grafts offered, or knee, joint or back problems, are created by the catabolic response to exhaustion when the body is so hyperaroused its catecholamine levels cause excessive endocrine and adrenalin secretions. To be invited off this particular edge and to look at one's relationship with life would give us a freer choice. Many cosmetic surgeries could also come into this category. It is time-consuming to go through these procedures, and many people live out their edge in the waiting rooms of doctors and hospitals. Sometimes, of course, this may be all that we can do, in which case we need to accept that this is so, and that it may be our only hope of a kind and touching hand.

In medicine we are being stretched into control issues. Should we fund transplants so that everyone may have the benefit of spare-part surgery? Wear out one heart, get another? Use a kidney and get another? The ethical dilemmas have never been so strong. So we swap one edge for another. If our desire for control has led us to develop machines that will take over life for us those machines, as well as perhaps giving us more life, are now posing deep questions about how and on what terms we live.

But if we cannot be informed and aware, we need to look at this process and take charge of where it could take us. It is harder to move about the edge with too many medications and operation scars.

FALLING ASLEEP AND SHUTTING DOWN

We all shut down inside when things get too much. It is a natural protection of the psyche that consciousness will be eclipsed when what is going on becomes unbearable and we have no learned mechanisms with which to deal with it. This has been well documented by recent studies of children who were abused by a trusted adult when young, and whose memories of the event remain hidden, often submerged within their bodies, presenting as physical symptoms or emerging in nightmares, phobia and chronic anxiety. It may be that for some of our time on the edge we just have to shut down, to protect ourselves, to give ourselves a break.

There is all the difference in the world between a conscious decision to shut down for a while and immerse oneself in a completely different activity from the vigilant demands of the daily edge, and simply giving up. Shutting down mindfully would be travelling to a new place, reading a novel, working at a garden, cooking, digging out a pond, or embroidery. The shut-down is a conscious displacement of energy by diversion into another mode of being. It is always surprising what comes out of it. Shut-down of the negative kind, which would constitute a wrong turning or a pitfall of the edge, would involve deciding to give up any idea of a spiritual quest and sell ourselves into its opposite, opting for literalization. Falling asleep means being lured by the spells offered by the false gods, being transported away like Sleeping Beauty so that we remain unconscious, awaiting the kiss of the prince. If we spend too long in a Sleeping

Beauty trance, we are vulnerable to any false god who dresses up as a prince. Too long flying like Peter Pan, avoiding contact with the ground, has the same effect. We are waiting, within our provisional life, for someone or something to take us out of it, hoping for magic. The edge then is the provisional life itself. The longer it goes on, the more likely we are to slide into bitterness or rage, to feel disappointed in the world that has failed us, and the more desperate may be our attachments to those others in whom we invest our hope.

Falling asleep may appear in the form of an avoidance trap which takes us on a circular route back into itself again. It is available to both conscious and unconscious aspects of ourselves. We may *need* to fall asleep at times when the reality of what is happening has become unbearable and it is our only protection. But we can keep a check on using avoidance as a habitual way of deferring responsibility or management of the pain of change. We only put off the moment of change, and this may be forced upon us by means we are even less able to tolerate than those we fear.

THE VOICE AND CONVERSATION OF SUICIDAL INTENT

This voice says, 'Death is the only answer. Give up now. You've taken more than you can bear. Nothing is worth it, and anyway, it doesn't matter. No one will notice. Your death won't make any difference.' The fantasy is that death is the solution to the problems of current life. The unknown is preferable to the known. Thoughts of death as a way out begin to arise in our waking moments, and our dreams may well be filled with masks of death, blind alleys, skulls and crossbones, coffins, corpses and dying animals and children. Sometimes our longing for death means that we neglect ourselves and our surroundings. The more we focus on the thoughts of death the more our energy supports the logic of our idea. Suddenly we find that we are thinking clearly about death and how to bring it about, and there may be some relief that we have found a solution. The more our ideas remain unspoken inner convictions, the more these ideas become inflamed into the illusion that death is the only answer.

Many people who have committed suicide successfully have only alluded to it in cryptic terms – 'I'd be better off out of the way', 'There's not much for me to hang around for' – or have begun to tidy up their affairs, reduced their lives' content or given up looking after themselves. And in an average social situation these comments or actions would be regarded uneasily and the person reassured, perhaps comforted, but the suicide inside would forge ahead without challenge. Only reality testing – telling someone what we are thinking, that we are thinking of killing ourselves – will bring the matter to a wider perspective where we gather *all* the facts. I have said throughout this journey on the edge that we should take a scientific approach, where all issues at stake are placed in evidence so that both the ego–personality and the wise self have the opportunity to comment. Choosing our own death is a very serious matter. It has been the choice of many, from the ill-fated lovers Romeo and Juliet to Ernest Hemingway, Virginia Woolf, Sylvia Plath, Arthur Koestler and Bruno Bettleheim, all deeply thinking and feeling people who we assume gave the matter a great deal of thought. But no one has returned from a successful suicide to tell us whether it actually brought the relief from pain it courted. And for the millions of Buddhists a suicidal act increases the karmic burden of the soul; for millions of Catholics it is a mortal sin. The result for both is to live with the burden of limbo, never knowing one's place.

When suicide becomes a seductive answer to the psychological pain of living, our own suffering takes centre stage and it is as if no one else exists. There are many delusions – that we are worthless and have become invisible to others because of our plight, that others must be made to suffer as we have and only in this way will we get even, that we cannot live unless we are perfect, and once fallen we can never arise, that our sense of loss is so acute we cannot tolerate the burden of feeling for a minute longer. The pain is that we are at these times unable to connect with a person or way of significance that gives our being meaning and a place in the world, which lights up our way. The illusion is that killing ourselves will take away the pain and our suicide will not make any difference to those about us.

What Is It That Becomes Dangerous?

All of us at times think about our own death, and for many the idea of death is seductive and a release from the difficulty of living a conscious life. One of the huge philosophical questions is why more people do not commit suicide, and what this tells us about the living. The most dangerous time for this question is when it is taken up literally by the logical ego and in isolation from other systems or people. If we spend too long listening only to the voice of the part of us that wants to die this voice becomes insistent, obsessional and secretive. The secret is part of the seduction, that no one knows what we have up our sleeve, and when they do we will be gone and will have triumphed. This is the hideous cut of the suicide thrust, because suicide always leaves a trail of unfinished business and misery for those who are left behind – unresolved feelings, guilt, skeletons in the cupboard to haunt those who come after.

Listening for the Note of the Suicide Within

What is this part and what is its character? What does it want, what would it say if it could? How can we give this part listening space and time so that we can make a proper assessment of whether suicide is appropriate for us? Suicide is not a soul decision but one of ego–personality. What is it the ego cannot stand that it wants to take everyone with it? Naming the unbearable psychological pain and being true witness to the suffering gives us powerful ammunition with which to enter this dialogue dance. Our conversation may carry on throughout the edge and through conversations of this kind we come closer to knowing our true will and basis for survival than at any other time. Only dialoguing will help these issues become clear.

Suicidal Thinking Can Become the Threshold

Realizing how far we are on the edge of life and death is frightening. It may frighten us into rethinking life. There is the cocoon time, when one feels isolated and alone, the world of tunnel vision which Al Alvarez calls the 'closed world of the suicidal being lived by forces I could not control, feeling inaccessible, remote, out of communication, impervious to anything outside the closed world of self destruction'. Once this tunnel vision is broken, usually by speaking of one's intent or offering the image of this closed world to another, or by something spontaneous that emerges on this edge between life and death, then something new begins to happen. Even if this is just time, it is time with a difference, time in which something else may be appraised. In his book *Darkness Visible*, William Styron writes movingly about being in this very place, when his thinking about ending his life had solidified and he had made preparation, even to the point of burying his diaries of torment among plastic bags in the dustbin outside, knowing the bin men called early the next morning. He sat alone in the living room in the early hours of the morning bundled up against the chill, having torn up his efforts to write a suicide note and forced himself to watch the tape of a film. At one point in the film the characters moved down the hallway of a music conservatory, beyond the walls of which, from unseen musicians, comes the soaring contralto from Brahms's *Alto Rhapsody*. He writes:

> This sound, like all pleasure, I had been numbly unresponsive to for months, pierced my heart like a dagger, and in a flood of swift recollection I thought of all the joys the house had known: the children who had rushed through its rooms, the festivals, the love and work . . . I realized all this was more than I could ever abandon.

The next day he was admitted to hospital.

Later on he describes linking the contralto voice with that of his mother who died when he was only nine, and to the unmanageable loss he had carried unconsciously for years, and which possibly contributes to the force behind the themes of the pain and loss of love in his many books, especially *Sophie's Choice*. The fact that the sound came from an unseen voice within the film seems particularly evocative, a voice calling him into life from the very edges of suicide, a voice which could well have come from a transpersonal or soul longing to be heard.

134

Part Four

STEPPING STONES AND SAFE PLACES FOR THE EDGE

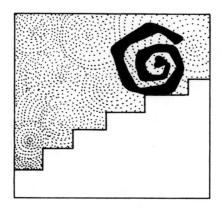

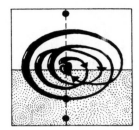

16

The Stepping Stones and How to Use Them

HONOUR YOUR IMAGES

Stick with the vessel or container you have chosen in your imagination to take you through the journey of the edge. Allow any images that have emerged for you during this mapping of the edge to be amplified by your life's experience and by the time that follows. Draw, paint, sculpt, dance, make poetry and keep a journal that honours the individual language of the place you are in. These recordings are the Ariadne thread that journeys with you during your time in this place. However banal or painful they may appear to you at the time, however depressed and painful the recordings may appear, however little you think you have to offer to any method of recording, trust in the method itself and time will be your reward. I am still astonished at what my personal journals still show me from the times I recorded as a reluctant, weary traveller. And time after time people share with me their own experience of these matters. When we read the details and smell the atmosphere through the recordings of where we have been, we marvel at just what we can come through, as well as our method of making records, and we marvel at the process that somehow carries on despite what is happening.

LOVE THE EARTH

Begin to get used to the earth's rhythms and seasons and trust in these, that everything has its own season and that your time on the edge will have its peaks and troughs and deepest, darkest places, and that the spring will arrive when the time is ready. It will not be at your will, but at the gestation of the time your individual journey takes that will show you the small green shoots of new life. When you begin to smell the turning of the earth within your own life you will know that you are ready to emerge into the spring dawn and that your ground will be wider with a harvest to come.

NEVER UNDERESTIMATE HOW MUCH WE CAN LEARN AND GO ON LEARNING

Psychology, perhaps because of the influence of psychoanalysis and its emphasis on past developmental thinking, has tended to underestimate just how much humans go on learning. Many of the cognitive therapies that are being widely used throughout the British National Health Service are based on this idea of change. When we can identify the negative beliefs that underpin our negative thinking and revise their emphasis, we can lessen the hold of negative or depressed thinking upon our way of life. This means that we can unlearn the unhelpful things we have learned which limit our life experience, and learn new ways of approaching both our inner and our outer lives. And it is never too late. Janet, in her mid-70s, found that she could begin to express herself affectionately for the first time in her life, having repressed her feelings for fear of their being misinterpreted. As she experimented, first with the children of her close neighbours, then with her cousin, she found that she could open up to her own warmth and that others welcomed it. I have found working with older age groups, and supervising other professionals who specialize in this work, some of the most moving and enlightening changes, changes that emerge just when the person is about to give up on themselves or be relegated to a rigid drug-controlled regime.

Just because we have encountered things in a certain way, it does not mean that they must be the same for ever. Once people decide to change and to tackle the aspects they have identified as getting in the way of their hopes, loves and joys, this force of intention can move mountains.

ACTIVE WAITING

Learn to become an acute listener to everything that happens around you. Pick up the signs that you know herald something of interest. Because of your journey on the edge you have a unique opportunity to tune in to the minutiae of your everyday functioning because your life by definition is narrowed down and you are likely to be much alone with your inner world. You can get to know your dreams, fantasies, thoughts, images, longings and body messages as well as the parts of life and people you find yourself drawn towards. You can get to know your own patterns and traits, you can become used to listening to the subtle messages of the day such as, 'This is a day for thinking and sorting out; this is a day for being with people; this is a day for being alone; this is a day for recording and listening to music; this is a day for searching out sacred texts and finding what has been written on the themes that are emerging for my own under-standing.' If you attune your ears to the finest of sounds, you will hear all that you need to hear. In *Peace Is Every Step*, Thich Nhat Hanh writes:

> Are you massaging our Mother Earth every time your foot touches her? Are you planting seeds of joy and peace? If we maintain awareness of our breathing and continue to practise smiling, even in difficult situations, many people, animals, and plants will benefit from our way of doing things.

DISCRIMINATION

Choose carefully all that you put before you – everything that you read, watch, hear, smell, touch. Become sensitive to the vibrations of all around you. *Everything* affects us, and there is growing evidence that we are affected on subtle energy levels by atmosphere, aura, others' vibrations, chemicals, sounds, things in the air, the presence of past and current bodies. Elaine told me of being visited in hospital after her collapse.

> I felt so vulnerable, as if I had no skin. Other people seemed to come straight at me, straight in. The nurses were one thing, they were

neutral, they had their official job. When my parents came and I saw their hurt and anger behind the forced smile I heard again that childhood cry, 'Elaine! not you again, what are you bothering us with this time?' In that moment I saw how I'd had to protect myself from their worry and fear, and their anger when I kept getting ill. I could see that they didn't know how to cope. And I saw, all at the same time, that I must learn to protect myself in different ways from the old ones of shutting myself off or getting ill. I closed my eyes after they had gone and imagined a thin blue silk cloak that went from covering my feet up to a hooded peak over my head. My skinless body at last had a veil, which did not shut anything out. I have stayed with this image and it still has enormous value for me today.

Vera wrote in her journal after receiving her first massage therapy following a long, disabling black depression.

I can sense that there are some healing hands coming my way. Through the massage I have located them physically. I know that these hands have been around somewhere throughout the last four years, in the doctors I've seen, the other patients I've met and in odd moments when I stopped to talk to someone in passing. Suddenly these fleeting images are becoming visceral. When I need to I can allow them.

FIND A WITNESS

A true witness is someone who will be there throughout your journey in the way most appropriate, who has the skills of the midwife, who knows when to trust in the process and let it take its course and when to call in other helpers. One of my workshop participants, herself a midwife, said to me, 'A midwife knows when to call in the experts *only* when bleeding occurs.' If you are going to bleed as part of your edge journey, and we have seen that the edge can be sharp, choose a skilled midwife who knows their craft. Get some help in the choosing if you are in doubt and trust your own feeling. Choose someone who will let you be and who will watch for you in times of danger, who will know how to name this danger and discuss it with you, always giving you the choice of the next step but also knowing when they must act for you in the ways appropriate.

FIND OTHERS WHO HAVE BEEN THERE BEFORE YOU

Choose from the ancient mythologies and stories from current literature and film, from modern heroic journeys and initiations and find a story, theme or sound which speaks to you and take it with you. Speak to the characters of those heroes and heroines, find all you can about them, let them stand as examples at the same time as honouring your own individual quest. And the people with whom you resonate may change as you change and your emphasis shifts. Allow for this, and for new characters to come into your awareness. Let them tell you about themselves.

LET THE VOICE OF THE SELF BE HEARD

Be silent often enough and court solitude so that you may hear your true self. None of us need to emulate others or copy more than is appropriate for new learning. When you feel your real self calling, always be ready to honour with your listening, however bizarre or unknown.

FEED YOUR SOUL

Find what for you is soul food – the language of the soul through music, poetry, beauty, dance, the written word or simply rhythms that honour the basic life of the soul. Read the texts which serve you in this way and return to them daily, perhaps writing them out to encourage you in the way of their beauty. Every day practise the values of a soul commitment.

WHO TO LISTEN TO

There are many people who offer advice and profound words today, many who would be a guru. Be careful. Listen to what is being said and the tone it carries. If it is too fervent, too controlling, too demanding, you need to stand back and ask questions.

Differentiate between passion which is needed as a source and the fervency that comes with being *too* intent in an ungrounded, lopsided way that tries to force its point. Take note of the example those whose words you may admire set by their own personal daily living. Someone who preaches peace and loving but who is warring arrogantly with their neighbours or manipulating outcomes is showing us a polarized picture, the Janus face. People who live by their own standards, ethics and principles down to the small minutia of how they behave in shops and bus queues, and who give generously to those who come their way, are true bounty. They live by what they say and their lives are living evidence of their belief and standards. Take a wide view and take many views.

The following quotation from Gautama Buddha was given by Professor Charles Tart at a conference in Cambridge:

> Do not believe in anything simply because you have heard it.
> Do not believe in traditions just because they have been handed down for many generations.
> Do not believe in anything because it is spoken and rumoured by many.
> Do not believe in anything because it is written in our religious books.
> Do not believe in anything merely on the authority of teachers and elders.
> But after observation and analysis when you find that anything agrees with reason and is conducive to the good and benefit of one and all accept it and live up to it.

Part Five

THE EDGE AS THRESHOLD TO TRANSFORMATION

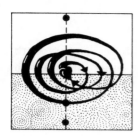

17

Paths of Initiation

So round about me shone a living light
Which left me wrapped in such a dazzling veil
That nothing else was visible to me.

'Always the love which makes this heaven restful
Receives all to itself with a like welcome,
To hold the candle ready for the flame.'

No sooner did I take in these few words
Than inwardly I understand that I
Was rising high above my human powers.

And I was so inflamed with the new vision
That – however luminous the light –
My eyes could have withstood the sight of it.

And I saw a light flowing like a river
Glowing with amber waves between two banks
Brilliantly painted by spellbinding spring.

Dante, *Paradisio*, Canto xxx, translated by James Cotter

Because the edge is such a difficult place to navigate there will be many moments when we think 'What is the point?' Our knowledge, the limitations of ego–consciousness and the ordinary levels of conscious awareness are not up to processing such a potentially major change in our being as the edge is offering. When something else is clearly afoot – and we know this because we will have tried all our known mechanisms of coping with change – we have to enter a period when we must find ways of surrendering to the process that is going on but which feels as if it is 'not of our own doing'. Our questions have to move from 'Why me?', 'Why now?', 'What have I done to deserve this?', 'It's not fair!', 'Now I've blown it!', to 'What is this (experience) saying?', 'What purpose does this (my feeling now) serve?', 'Who can I speak to about this?', or simply 'Please help me, whoever is out there.' These times mean that what is happening to us on an unconscious level is more important than what is happening on the conscious level.

Our relationship with the self within us and this connection to the greater collective Self is what is at stake. We cannot find this self without an edge and the properties it creates. Any offering we can make to this in terms of recording and working with our dreams, keeping a journal of our random thoughts and feelings, working with the images that draw us into the non-rational levels of awareness, will be serving the unconscious call for recognition. We must journey in the dark and as we do so we develop different ways of seeing and sensing, we hear sounds we had not heard before, smell new fragrances, meet the figures that live in the dark that have something to tell us.

There will be times when we will actually give up trying to process our way through it as conscious brave warriors and we will long for the relief of unconsciousness. This may involve trying to lose our pain and misery in some mindless pursuit – drugs, drink, television, sex, shopping, oblivion. We cannot be vigilant all the time and so we have to make resting places within our edge and get lost for a while, and then take up the conscious thread of the edge path again.

Throughout this book we have been describing the edge as having the potential for profound inner change and for the transformation of one way of being into another. The overall metaphor for this journey of the edge is initiation. With the metaphor of initiation come structures which allow us to make sense of the different aspects of the journey and give us permission actively to engage in their meanings. Our modern resting places or cul de sacs, entered into knowingly not blindly, can then take the place of the initiation rites that were once a vital

146

part of the structure of human social life, giving a shape and a dignity to the passage from one state or way of being into another. The fact that we may not see this process until we are caught up in it or beyond it does not matter. We see it when we need to.

SEEING THE THRESHOLD

An example of the 'seeing' that often heralds the initiate's journey comes from a man I saw during a period of crisis who suffered from terrible boils; they kept appearing despite countless courses of antibiotics. He felt that he was being punished like Job for something he had done, but was unclear what it could be. He experienced that suffering of depression and exhaustion into which we can sink when we have nowhere else to go. He felt that what was happening to him was unfair, unjust. In his bitterness he felt compelled to drive on, overworking, unable to rest, and he fixed all his nervous energy upon a need to take revenge for his life's losses. Part of his treatment for the boils was to take a salt bath three times a day, to let the salty water bathe his back and buttocks, where the worst crop of boils were. He had to buy common salt in large quantities and prepare his baths, then sit in them for 15 minutes each day. He thought: 'This is what *she* has brought me to', referring to his ex-wife, and he commented on the bitter taste his wife's leaving had left in his mouth and the suffering this had caused him. The salt baths involved a laborious procedure, one which grounded him, but he complied with it, like a dutiful martyr. Then one day he mentioned how the salt had glistened as he measured it out and how amazing it was that such a simple, common substance was his treatment in a time of highly sophisticated antibiotics. When asked what the salt baths meant to him, he replied thoughtfully; 'It's a bit like some sort of ritual isn't it?' Then the naming of the ritual and what it might be preparing him for awakened his curiosity. It became the thread that took him further in investigating the ancient properties of salt itself. 'They are the salt of the earth', he would say about those people who were befriending him. He began reading about salt, that it is an ancient substance that links us with all the elements, that it is vital to life, that the balance of the salts within the cellular structure are the key to molecular life. He read that salt was an arcane substance, associated with sea water and the process of baptism, and he was encouraged to read Jung and the alchemical writings on the subject of salt and the saltings.

What came out of this for him was his need to examine the substance of bitterness. He had been left by his wife, who had gone off with his best friend and he was crazed with grief and jealousy. He had thrown himself into work in his own business, exhausting himself, eating badly and getting drunk at weekends. He came to see the boils as symbols of something trapped, angry and poisonous locked inside him. He became more consciously aware of his consuming bitterness and desire for revenge, how much his drive to get even by taking out his fury and destruction on himself could cost him dearly in terms of relating. As he caught its reality on the wave he became more in touch with a much deeper level of grief for the loss of his wife as a person and the marriage they had shared and some of the quality of the things he wanted from intimacy with another. He saw that the boils had alerted him to a choice: he could become like the closed, angry weals of his boils – septic, full of pus and fury, erupting and raging at the unfairness of fate and losing himself in his wretched bitterness. (The expression 'to lose oneself' is useful here, because our sense of self is what is at stake.) Or he could engage in the salty process of self-preservation (salt is also a preservative), by expressing all that he felt inside about the loss of his wife, to wash the wounds and cleanse them by his daily baptisms, to weep salt tears for what was lost and to begin a process of intimacy with himself. This movement – from bitterness to acceptance and the ensuing wisdom to be gained – he saw as his personal initiation.

Pushed to the edge, all we can do is to pay attention to the needs of the self that is calling to us. In *Mysterium Coniunctionis*, Jung writes:

> Bitterness and wisdom form a pair of alternatives; where there is bitterness wisdom is lacking, and where wisdom is there can be no bitterness. Tears, sorrow, and disappointment are bitter, but wisdom is the comforter in all psychic suffering.

Just this movement, from the tunnel vision of revenge to seeing his movingly created boils as a symbol of both his distress and the departure point for a new relationship with the self, allowed him to change the lens on his struggle to that of an initiatory journey. He was being offered both a way to *be* within the actual situation and a way forward with choices. And the process seemed to be directed to a complete change in his attitude to relating, both to himself and to others. His movement was from the position of holding on and controlling that which he desired to opening the way for the true expression of his own feelings in relation to himself. Ultimately he made the shift in attitude from potential bitterness to wisdom.

NAMING THE EDGE AS AN INDIVIDUAL INITIATION PATH

The journey of the edge involves many extremes: the properties described in part two, the pitfalls in part three, and the need to develop the images, the threads and the stepping stones that offer us a helping hand as we stumble and weave our way, sometimes over a period of years. We can see that the edge itself represents a path common to the process of initiation where the individual initiate undergoes the tasks, tests and waiting common to all initiatory journeys. The actual naming of the way of initiation is important. This may be named as such by someone else, someone who knows us and perhaps has an idea of where we have come from and are going to. Or it may be a wise person, a priest, an older person such as a grandmother, a friend, a teacher, a therapist or a group leader. Or our moment of seeing, insight and naming might be from the woman who hangs her washing in the next-door garden. In *Forms of Feeling*, Robert Hobson quotes from Joseph Conrad to describe the moments of seeing and naming.

> My task which I am trying to achieve is . . . to make you hear, to make you feel . . . it is, before all, to make you see. That – and no more, and it is everything . . . that glimpse of truth for which you have forgotten to ask.

149

In whatever form the pointer to initiation comes, naming this process is of huge value in terms of consciousness, for when we accept this path we shift to be in readiness for it, instead of fighting against it. The point is that we become ready for the moment of knowing. Once it is formally named we then have the blueprint that helps shape our experience. Then we create and connect with the thread or light to keep hold of as the going gets tough. In the process of initiation we become the hero or heroine setting out on a quest and we take on the gravity and enormity of such a venture. To accept our edge as such a path means dignifying the process and joining forces with all the other heroes and heroines who have come this way. We will not be alone. The words and images of others who have been this way can guide us. They will not be exactly the same, for modern initiations are about the time we are in, but they will have many resonances with the mythological and historical figures who have left us their words and footprints.

Dante, seeing an unknown figure as he stumbled about called: 'Have pity on me whatever thou art or very man or ghost.' His figure turned out to be the poet Virgil, who became Dante's guide through the first two stages of his journey, until Virgil handed him over to Beatrice with the words: 'Now let pleasure be your guide.' We may meet internal figures who speak or whisper to us in phrases or words that puzzle. And these all form threads that we take into the labyrinth of the journey of the edge as we accept its initiatory task and take this into our own hearts. The idea that this journey is about something and can have a creative or positive outcome because of what we make of it during the travel can deepen and strengthen the thread that carries us through. However flimsy the thread and however many times it gets lost, it is none the less as vital as the thread Ariadne held for Theseus in the Underworld. The people that name this thread or light our way as we stumble along become our wise elders or talismans, those who know something we do not yet know, or have been on their own initiatory paths and can shine their light on ours. These people may well be everyday folk we meet only once, or in passing, or they may become firm friends and guides. They speak with the knowing of those who have travelled far, and their language is seamed with the wisdom that is enough to ignite our imagination.

150

The gift of true wisdom is that it does not tell anyone what to do or how to do it nor does it speak in literal terms as if this were this and that were that. The musical tone sounded by the wise friends we meet at the place of the edge will outshine anything we have known before because their quality will resonate with the music of our own being. It is at these times that, if we are open to receive it, people, stories, images and examples of those who have travelled before us are the beacons in the dark, the footprints in the desert, the friendly hand coming into the well, the kindness amongst the harsh rocks. And there are also those figures in mythological or world history who have described being on the edge as an initiate's path and recorded their journey and findings for us to read as our turn comes around.

STAGES OF THE INITIATION PATH

Put simply, initiation means the act of origination into the new. When we initiate something we start, open, get something going. To be an initiate means that we place ourselves within the process of learning something new and follow a custom or ancient practice that has been recorded throughout the ages. The initiation journey we have been looking at in this book concerns the invitation from the edge to become mindful and conscious of what we are doing and to turn away from the pull to remain unconscious in order to individuate into the sacred purpose of our life. The goal, or outcome, is to develop a fuller relationship with the self that has us and to live life in service to this self and away from the demanding pull of the limited ego–self.

The way of initiation will vary and the thresholds are many. Some of us are initiated into a new relationship with ourselves by a relationship we make (like C S Lewis), by following a religious belief (St John of the Cross, the Lord Buddha), by a programme of study (as in *Educating Rita*, where the process of academic learning moved Rita away from her old life into something new), by a long illness, an accident, or a near-death experience.

We may have felt tense and unhappy for a number of years and know that something is wrong but be unsure how to name it. We may simply feel that we have outgrown the set of personality

151

clothes we have been wearing and need to discard them to move into others that represent the next phase of our being, or of our life.

The spiral maps in part one show us the progression from child to adolescence, adulthood, maturity and wisdom, and each of these stages is entered through a process of initiation, where something has to die in order to give space and life to something newly developing. James Hillman writes: 'It is illusory to hope that growth is but an additive process requiring neither sacrifice nor death. The soul favours the death experience to usher in change.' Most of us are called to become initiated into carrying out different tasks such as the movement from son or daughter to adult, parent, grandparent; from disciple, acolyte or hand-maiden to teacher or leader; from innocent abroad to mature, responsible person engaged with life. Those who are unable to accept the call to initiation can feel stuck or in limbo, living only in their child or adolescent spiral and feeling cut off from the wider, deeper experiences a relationship with the inner life can offer. The self may begin to call us to do its work, by forcing us to sacrifice ego desires so that we must find a way of true relation-ship with the self that has us. Or we may just wake one day like Dante, and feel we are in a dark wood where all is wholly lost and gone. Some may call this depression, or mid-life crisis, or even psychosis, but whatever it is called it may be carrying our initia-tory experience. And it may well be some time before we move into seeing it in that way. When we do, we will have crossed from one side of the river of life to the other and our geography will be different, as will what we need from that place.

The processes of initiation will all be individual, but having a blueprint for the initiatory journey means that we are able to share certain ingredients and to follow a pattern.

1   *Feeling lost and in alien territory*

The first stage seems to be losing that which has been familiar and finding ourselves in alien territory. Then there is the process where everything that has gone before does not work any more. The tendency is to try and hold on, to find a 'cure', especially today when cures are on offer. We may have to make many detours and experiments in terms of approaches to what might be the nature of our suffering or strange new condition. But we tend to end up alone, having to make of it the best we can and use the resources that only we are able to recruit and which work for us. Then we make our stumbling way on alien territory, where we learn as we go.

2   Crisis

Crisis tends to be related to extremes such as bleeding, accident, emergency. Crisis certainly represents a turning point when before and after are in acute tension and in an unknown space. Internally, crises only tend to occur when our store of knowledge or wisdom runs out and we are in a completely new place, when we simply have no more reserves to call upon to help guide us. And we have already seen that crisis is both danger and opportunity. It is internally that feeling of being in something new and alien where nothing that has gone before can be called upon to help us to cope. The danger is that we will collapse ourselves into this place. The opportunity is for something new to come in. Even the act of having to ask for help and being able to accept being helped or looked after is very new to people who are determined never to be vulnerable. And in the new we can often find the seeds of potential for change in attitude. Crises tend to happen at times when we feel brittle or rigid inside, when we are unable to be flexible or dance to the rush of demand upon us. Many people who have attained maturity and wisdom tend not to have crises as such but will speak of times of extremes where they are called upon to focus particular attention.

We tend to be 'plunged' into crisis, but we may also realize that we have gradually been sliding closer to actual crisis when some of our habits or patterns are mirrored back to us. One person said to me:

> I hadn't realized how I'd been neglecting my body until a friend stayed with me and I had only stale food to offer her. I was shocked – and so was she – to face this. I had been totally preoccupied in keeping myself going each day to the job I hated that all my energy was spent. Her visit prompted me to ask for some leave so that I could address just what was happening to me physically. Of course this

meant getting into my feelings, all the feelings I'd put on hold. But the crisis initiated me into quite a different attitude to self-care, and to giving time for feelings to come in.

And on another note, someone described to me the sad aftermath of her husband's death and how she felt she would never pick herself up again to face life on her own.

> I'd got used to lighting a candle in the mornings and putting it on an old chest where I also kept precious books, letters and objects such as stones and shells. This friend said, 'Are you mourning or preparing for something?' and I realized that inside I was getting in a state of readiness for my next phase, after my husband's death. So I had been mourning but was also preparing, and I had this feeling that each day I was offering something up to the universe, and in turn it was speaking to me.

3 Testing out

Some people speak of their 'trials by fire', of their 'passage on the long sea journey', of their being 'brought to their knees'. Part of the journey of initiation is that we are tested out on our true mettle, the true mettle of who we really are. We may feel tested again and again, until we scream out, 'Not this *again*.' Sometimes it is when we have lost sight of ourselves and the path we are on, when all is given up and we feel forsaken by everyone and everything that has had meaning for us, that the dawn begins to break and a new awareness begins to assert itself. In this process the rough, redundant, inappropriate coatings are burned or washed off. The base substances of the ego–personality are stressed and stretched, placed in the great cauldron or the vast alchemical flask for the forging process of change to take place. There are many examples of this in our ancient myths and religious texts, for example the testing through temptation of Christ in the wilderness. Psyche was also tested during her quest for her lost lover Cupid, whom she had dared to look at whilst he was sleeping. Her subsequent voyage into the underworld, described by Apuleus in *The Golden Ass*, takes her to gather wool from wild sheep with poisonous horns in a dangerous valley, but she is assisted by a green reed; when she has to sort out the mixed seeds of lentils, beans, poppy seed and millet by morning, an army of ants help her all night. And in *The Magic Flute* the lovers Papageno and Papagena have to undergo the tests and trials of silence, blindfolding and mistaken identity to prove their commitment to love.

We may dream of having to climb a mountain, pass through a narrow gully or over a rope bridge, make our way across the ocean or a swirling river, cross a border without a map or passport or wander anxiously through a maze or labyrinth. If we experience our testings as fire, our images may well be of burning; if our images are watery we will feel awash with feeling or as if we could weep for ever; we might be caught in imagery connected to the earth, such as feeling entombed, trapped, held in a womb-like cave with all the lights out. One way to experience this testing is to work with the imagery to literally feel your way with the quality and property of the image as your guide. At the beginning of this book we looked at the four functions of feeling, thinking, sensing and intuition. If we give each of these functions a corresponding image of water, air, earth and fire, we can perhaps feel what function we are being most tested on. For example, if we feel we are in a dark cave with all the lights out we will have to move about very carefully, probably on our hands and knees, and go about tapping walls, smelling things and listening hard for the subtlest of sounds. If we are used to seeing clearly, having the lights on in our life and seeing where we are going, this test will be for us to develop other ways of seeing and hearing. If we feel we are in a deep river or tossed about at sea when we are used to having our feet on firm ground we will have to learn to become swimmers and pearl divers. If we feel we have been thrown up in the air like a bird without wings we will have to learn about safe flight – perhaps about expressing our thoughts and ideas in a clearer, airy way.

Some images of initiation are of being blindfolded so that we cannot see in the old way. Our usual methods of communication are blocked so that others have to grow. This is the test. The testing makes us question what is being asked of us and what purpose it serves, rather than trying to return things to the way they were. The test has no examiners but ourselves, and passing through the levels of testing automatically seems to bring us into new levels of awareness. If we fail to acknowledge the test and to move into open questioning, we can get very stuck. It is then that our fears increase and our need for literalization to provide concrete answers gets in the way of our asking and listening. Our images begin to fade and our imagination dries up, its energy fuelling obsession with control and change at any cost. If we fasten our feelings on what has not happened for us, on our unlived life, or on our disappointments with other people who have let us down, we will remain in a psychological limbo. And it can be tempting. It is easier in one way to blame our miseries or incapacities on what has not happened than to brave it through to something not yet known. And we desperately need the inspiration of the structures as laid down in ancient rites and stories to guide us, so that we can fully claim the hero or heroine within us and all the energy needed for the work. In *The Hero with a Thousand Faces*, Joseph Campbell writes:

> The psychological dangers through which earlier generations were guided by the symbols and spiritual exercises of their mythological and religious inheritance, we today (in so far as we are unbelievers, or, if believers, in so far as our own inherited beliefs fail to represent the real problems of contemporary life) must face alone, or at best, with only tentative, impromptu, and not very effective guidance. This is our problem as modern, 'enlightened' individuals, for whom all gods and devils have been rationalized out of existence.

Part of initiation is to be tested by means of having things stolen from us, ripped away by the tricksterish Mercury, or coming off a pedestal, falling from a great height, and we may find that we are highly accident prone. The overall effect of all the means of testing is that we are being humbled, and our old survival ways of coping are being removed. The triumph of initiation is that we move into receiving all that our life brings as if it were a gift. We do not hold on to old structures which are being made redundant, nor do we make structures and excuses out of a mythological or psychological understanding, for it is possible to use the naming of the process as an excuse to escape from actual risk of engagement. People who say 'That was my shadow', or 'I've worked through my feminine, my father/mother complex', or who lean on some abstract or theoretical structure as an explanation for their behaviour, may well be missing the point of the actual surrender needed for initiation to show us its most golden aspects. The hardest test perhaps is that we actually do not know where we are going or what this travelling will bring us into, and we need to stay with this not-knowing as a vital part of our commitment. Later the appropriate shape and words will be able to be born.

4   *The dark night of the soul*

The night sea journey and the dark night of the soul are graphic images for the long, protracted experience of the initiation process. In Chapter 14, we looked at many of the questions and issues that come alive when nothing seems to be shifting or changing in our internal or external life. We have to undergo periods of seclusion, isolation or the monotony of long, repetitive hard graft. The metaphor of the dark night can help us to conceptualize where we are, and to join in with those heroes and heroines who have travelled this journey and survived to become wise commentators as we have encountered so far in this book such as Jung, Dante, Goethe and Picasso. Picasso's dark night of the soul, or *nekya*, came in his early twenties after his closest friend committed suicide. Then he entered his 'blue period' of melancholy and depression, mourning for his friend and the loss of life. He painted sad pierrots and harlequins, those mythical and carnival figures who carry so much of the language and pathos of being between two worlds, and towards the end of this seven-year stage he began to paint the mother and child images, as perhaps his psyche was emerging with the birth of a new life.

5   *Suffering*

In Buddhist thought the Four Noble Truths are firstly the 'reality of suffering', secondly that 'suffering can be overcome', then the 'analysis of suffering' and the practices we may develop to overcome suffering. Many of the causes of suffering come from ignorance, and the suffering which puts us closest to the edge is our overattachment to the rational or to blame as an explanation for our suffering and our ignorance of a transpersonal self.

How can we view the suffering that we must all become

engaged in without falling into a victim mentality? It seems vitally important not to disappear into suffering as a cause, or to identify oneself too strongly with suffering as an escape from real responsibility. If suffering means the struggle between what we feel we would like and what actually comes our way then it is an edge to be danced upon for the purpose of gaining balance. Some suffering of this kind has always been necessary for the gaining of strength and of growing up in terms of growing wise. But suffering is all too often looked upon as punishment for misdeeds or sin; as the work of some witch or devil who has put spokes into an image or stuck pins onto our photograph. And then there are those who parade their suffering daily in our newspapers, with the often common denominator of wanting to allocate blame and seek rescue. Martyrish suffering of the 'holier than thou' kind often hides an angry masochism and invites cold brutality. When suffering is entered into blandly, passively, without thought of proper engagement with what is happening, it is hard to find the heart to meet it. When suffering is entered into actively, consciously, it means we take it up gladly as the cutting edge to change, and then by its silent acceptance it speaks louder than any trumpet blast or pitying photograph.

Conscious suffering means accepting the yoke or mantle that has been given to us and deciding to choose it because it has already chosen us.

6 Initiation rites and rites of passage

Initiation rites are an ancient phenomenon embedded within every culture but possibly today much disguised or completely absent in Western nations. The traditional rites induce and channel suffering in order to create the threshold between emergent states of being or developing stages of life. The rites offer a ritualized loss of control and organization of chaos, recognizing that these aspects are important ingredients in the process of change and development in the human psyche.

Religious culture carries initiation rites for those who take holy vows and the steps into initiation as priests, monks or nuns. For those committed to a religious tradition in everyday life there are also the initiation rites into the body of the Church of confirmation and first communion, and within the Jewish culture the Barmitzvah which celebrates the emergence of the child both into the next phase of life and into their spiritual awareness and commitment. The process involves following a creed as laid down by scripture and being guided by a person who knows these scriptures well and who has themself undergone the appropriate initiatory rites.

The timing of initiation rites of passage frequently coincides with major social and physiological changes such as the rites surrounding birth, with the midwives making preparation for the process of labour and the delivery of a new-born child. Following birth there are many customs of welcoming and blessing a new child whilst 'heaven lies above us in our infancy' as Wordsworth wrote. The pagan ceremony of churching – presenting the new child to Mother Earth at a crossroads – was developed by the formal Western church into the 'churching' of women after childbirth. They were not allowed outside until they and their child had been presented into church and to God, after the 40-day 'quarantine'.

Menstruation rites, which have now completely disappeared in Western culture, celebrate the biological emergence of a girl into womanhood and link together the bodily reality of ovulation and fecundity with the spiritual sense of wonder at the potential for procreation. Rather than rejoicing today, most girls greet this occurrence with the idea that now they have the 'dreaded curse'. There are also seclusion rites in the Masai for menstruating women who have permission to withdraw and be alone, away from the company of men – possibly a relief all round and perhaps a successful approach to PMT.

Circumcision in Masai culture is undertaken by boys at puberty when they feel ready. It is highly ritualized, with several spectators in a public space. The boy stares at his mother throughout – it can take up to five minutes without any kind of anaesthetic – and she screams his agony for him. He must remain silent. After circumcision the boy becomes a warrior and lives on the edge of the bush with other boys away from the village. A later ritual ceremony within Masai culture is the *eunoto* annual festival in which warriors graduate to junior elders. They perform the famous high jumping dance for hours; the jumping induces a trance through hyperventilation. It is also a ritual time for taking drugs boiled from the roots of tree bark. This process marks a ritual and rite of passage in the life of the warriors, who then go on to acquire wives and cattle.

Perhaps our boiled-down equivalent of these socially organized and contained ceremonies takes the form of the acid trances, the raves and the sharing of crack among young people looking for a way to lose themselves and emerge different, or as new. But however these 'rites' are attempted, we have limited their naming into the pathologies of addiction, where the containment for chaos and loss of control is a detoxification unit or prison cell, and where most of the ritualized sharing takes place in drab basements or lavatories, or is lost altogether.

Then there are the rites of passage involving withdrawal from the general tribe, being alone and surviving nights in the desert or bush, and the blooding and sharing of secret passwords before entry into the next clan or group.

Dancing and chanting, drumming, fasting, bathing in water and the Dionysian and Bacchanalian rites of drunkenness and sexual orgy all offer the experience of rites of passage when changes in consciousness are required to bring about the movement from one level to another. These are not the cul de sacs mentioned earlier but rites organized, established and provided safely by experienced elders as an important container for the often dangerous and lonely process of change.

7   *The importance of ritual*

In part four we discussed the importance of regular ritual as a practice for the stepping stones for the edge. When we ritualize something we invest that moment with importance and meaning and we offer the opportunity for soul-gathering, for sacred energy to emerge. It is via the ritualization of events that they become sacred, precious. It may be simply the ritual of bathing each day, of meditation, of creating a meal or a fire. Making it into a ritual means that we invest the moment with more thought and energy that we would when we do things by rote, as a chore. Creating our own rituals for being on the edge means engaging in the meaning of the process of initiation, making it work for us, like the man with the salt baths, the woman with her candle, and others with their campfires keeping the flame alight to light the way, or those with sacred waters who seek a blessing for their crossing. There are rituals of prayer, meditation, chanting, singing, sharing silent walks with friends, building with stones like Jung, or painting out one's innermost passage like the many artists who leave their works for us to share. We do not have to be 'expert' artists, writers or poets, but we can let our own unique inner artistry weave its way via the ritualization to bear witness to our engagement with the sacred process going on within.

8 Death and rebirth

Part of initiation involves the experience of death and rebirth. The death may be an actual death, in the form of something or someone to whom we are attached, it could be the death of a part of ourselves that has outlived its usefulness, or it may be in the form of a living death, the feeling that we are still living biologically but are psychologically or emotionally dead. Stanislav Grof, whose pioneering work with the impact of prenatal experience on our consciousness, memory and capacity is recorded in his writing and research, says in *The Stormy Search for the Self*:

> The 'dying' and the agony during the struggle for rebirth reflect the actual pain and vital threat of the biological birth process. The ego death that precedes rebirth is the death of our old concepts of who we are and what the world is like, which were forged by the traumatic imprint of birth. As we are purging these old programmes by letting them emerge into consciousness they are becoming irrelevant and are, in a sense, dying. As frightening as this process is, it is actually very healing and transforming.

Grof goes on to name the sense of annihilation common to death and rebirth experiences, many of which we have been exploring in the properties of the edge. It could come through a sense of emotional disaster, intellectual and philosophical defeat, ultimate moral failure, even spiritual damnation – as if all reference points for our life are being destroyed. It seems that once we have

161

surrendered to this process as part of our initiatory experience and are prepared to undergo the trauma involved – not dissimilar to the surrender of the shaman to the unconscious processes necessary for healing, sometimes wounding and maiming themselves to induce the pain and suffering needed to alter the level of conscious awareness and to enter completely the intimate space of the person suffering – we can be reborn. All these ways, recorded in the ancient rites, stories, patterns and myths of many different cultures, show how death and rebirth is the most potent image for all major experiences. When we accept death as part of life with no divisions, we allow something else to come in, we allow the new, the dawn to be heralded.

The process is one of accepting that some aspect within our outer or inner life is dying and needs to be allowed to die. This is often hard for us because we cannot see beyond the immediate death and we fear there will be nothing beyond.

If we look into nature we see many examples of death and rebirth, from the savage pruning we give to rose trees and other plants to the burn of the autumn glow as if in a last fire before surrender to the dark of winter, followed by the emergence in spring of astonishing pale green new shoots of such vigour out of the old stubborn wood that we wonder where the strength lies. However much our earth has been plundered and pillaged, it still sends up these wonders.

9 Peak experience and unitive consciousness

The goal of initiation is that we pass through the different stages and emerge into another place that is waiting for us. This place may not be distinguishable from other geography we have known externally, but its feel will be very different. The way this place is experienced by different people varies hugely. Some actually see a great light, feel a surge of passion or an intense feeling of wellbeing, begin to feel truly alive for the first time in years, are aware that their attention span is more intense than ever before. Sometimes there is a sense of radiance within and without that is like a permanent smile.

Peak experience refers to those moments when we move beyond our everyday awareness and into a state of 'wholeness' or cosmic awareness. People describe these times as being enlightened into something beautiful and whole, where the entire world is seen in its fullness and vivid colours, where every sensation is felt absolutely. Some of these experiences last just moments, others hours or days, and after the intense period is over the person moves about the world with their consciousness permanently changed. These times are perhaps the nearest we come to an experience of wholeness and of being united with the entire universe. We may experience a profound sense of the inner marriage – the coming together of masculine and feminine consciousness which leads us into the path of wisdom, when we speak with both masculine and feminine aspects, when we are in balance, in the rhythm of the eternal dance. When people come into this place within themselves, the warmth and light and sense of groundedness – the sense of being truly present – tends to spread out to others. People with this light, who may have literally 'seen the light', will tend to shine like a beacon in their attractiveness. For it is something of this light, this knowing, this level of acceptance, that we all yearn for. The smile on the beatific face of His Holiness the Dalai Lama tells of this light, and so do many of the enigmatic, beatific lit-up faces that painters such as Michelangelo, Leonardo and Vermeer have given us. It was a face such as this on the nine-year-old Beatrice that initiated Dante into his great mythic and poetic adventure.

These experiences bring us more fully into the body of man- and womankind and into the animate world itself. In this way our life becomes dedicated to the wider purposes of living and, particularly today, to our survival on earth. It is not limited just to our own purposes but offers a way of being that could unite us within the brother- and sisterhood of humankind.

10   Awakening

After a long journey, particularly one with the sharp edges we have been exploring, we feel tired and yet awake. Often we feel childlike because we are approaching our life with the new-found wonder akin to that we first experience in childhood. We may have had transcendent and numinous experiences which still feel fresh. We feel more than ever like an initiate, but an initiate to the self and to life. And our life goes on. The shop on the corner is still the same but it somehow looks different. The friends and foes we are used to grappling with on a Monday morning are still there but we speak to them differently and some of them speak differently to us. It is like the Zen story of the monk looking for enlightenment who travelled far and wide in his search for the Master who would teach him. After crossing many mountains and rivers he finally came to a place where there lived a great and wise Master. The monk was given food at the kitchen and waited for his audience. When he had responded to the Master's question about his search and his journey, and after describing the dangers, the animals, the dangerous crossings on his way, the Master said to him: 'You must be tired after such a long journey, have you yet eaten?' When the monk replied that he had the Master said, 'Then go wash your bowl.'

Before enlightenment we chop wood. After enlightenment we chop wood. Everything has changed inside, and yet nothing has changed. There are still chores to be done, people to attend to, letters to answer and tasks to be planned. But we come to them in a very different way. Life does not get easier, nor does it get nicer, more problem-free, but our attitude to our engagement with our own life has changed dramatically. We come through something and we emerge as ourselves, able to listen to our own wise selves inside, not needing to be gurus or evangelists, but we speak from our own hearts as and when we find things and as we see things. We may see the world with fresh eyes, with a regained innocence and sense of wonder, delight and joy, and with our ability to receive the awe-inspiring aspects of creation fresh and marvelling. And because we have survived the darkest, rockiest, storm-tossed ride we owe a debt to the mysteries of the dark. In the same way that Persephone ate pomegranate seeds in the Underworld, signifying that she must return there for a proportion of every year in winter, so we must make a promise to let the darkness speak to us as and when it needs and to remain in awe at the relevation of the dark's own mysteries.

Life is found at the edge, and out of our struggle with the edge more life is born. There is great life to be had in our struggle between the ego–personality that has one limited set of thoughts and the self that has us, that is trying to emerge in order to connect us more deeply with our soul and to forge our spirit. When we have been touched by a powerful, numinous experience it is instantly recognizable. It may be this transcendent experience that ends our suffering or changes our attitude to suffering so that life is never the same again. The great and mighty mystery of life waits for all of us to stumble into it. We are awakened by these experiences into a more powerful connection with what for us is divine. Like a rich nectar it can feed our soul all our days, whatever, wherever we have to be. We may plan less and fret much less, we may be able to ride the huge storms knowing that they too will pass, and that it is not a question of getting through and onto the next stage, of planning when things are going to be over so that we can enjoy ourselves, it is our sacred relationship with the here and now of life that is our finest achievement.

Sun rises
at ground level
orange arc breaking grey ocean line
silent beauty

I stretch my hand to a warm face
tasting salt
breathing in the fine spray
washed from the worlds waters.

In the wind something is fresh.
Spores from the arms of trees
bring life into the forest
black auk can begin
winging its way to far off places.
The ploughed fields are emboldened
with the hard beauty of night frost.
And the pale green shoot of awakeing snowdrop is fearless
Life is returned to what it should be
allowing hope to turn the lens
and the green meadow glows.

Further Reading

This section lists books which have been mentioned in the text of the book, as well as other works which I have consulted, and which may contribute to supportive reading.

Abram, David, *The Spell of the Sensuous: Perception and Language in a More than Human World*, Pantheon Books, New York, 1996

Alvarez, Al, *The Savage God: a Study of Suicide*, Penguin Books, Harmondsworth, 1974

Campbell, Joseph, *An Open Life*, Larson, 1988
—— *The Hero with a Thousand Faces*, Bollingen, 1968

Cooper, J C, *An Illustrated Encyclopedia of Traditional Symbols*, Thames & Hudson, London, 1982

Dallet, Janet O, *Saturday's Child*, Inner City Books, Toronto, 1991

Dante, *The Divine Comedy*, translated by Dorothy Sayers, Penguin, London

Edinger, Edward, *Anatomy of the Psyche: Alchemical Symbolism in Psychotherapy*, Open Court, 1985
—— *Ego and Archetype*, Penguin, Baltimore, 1973

Egum, Anne, *The Frieze of Life: A Biographical Note on Edvard Munch*, National Gallery Publications, London, 1993

Estees, Clarissa Pinkola, *Women Who Run with the Wolves*, Ballantine Books, New York, 1992

Fontana, David, *The Lotus in the City: How to Combine Spiritual Practice with Everyday Life*, Element, Shaftesbury, 1995

Fontana, David, and Ingrid Slack, in *The Psychologist*, June 1996

Grof, Stan and Christina, *The Stormy Search for the Self*, Thorsons, London, 1990

Harpur, Patrick, *Daimonic Energy: A Field Guide to the Otherworld*, Viking Arkana, London, 1994

Hillman, James, *Anima*, Spring Publications, Dallas, Texas, 1985

—— *Suicide and the Soul*, Spring Publications, Zurich, 1964

Hillman, James (ed), *Puer Papers*, Spring Publications, Zurich, 1986

Hillman, James, and Michael Meade, *The Rag and Bone Shop of the Heart: Poems for Men*, Harper Perennial, 1992

Hobson, Robert F, *Forms of Feeling: The Heart of Psychotherapy*, Routledge, London, 1985

Jung, C G, *Commentary on the Kundalini Yoga*, Spring Publications, Zurich, 1932

—— *On the Psychology of the Trickster Figure: Collected Works, Vol 9, Part 1*, Routlege, London, 1959

Leonard, Linda Schierse, *Witness to the Fire: Creativity and the Veil of Addiction*, Shambala, New York, 1990

Lerner, Harriet Goldhor, *The Dance of Anger*, Harper & Row, New York, 1985

Lewis, C S, *A Grief Observed*, Faber, London, 1960

Lubin, Albert J, *Stranger on the Earth: A Psychological Biography of Vincent Van Gogh*, Holt, Reinhart & Winston, New York, 1972

Luke, Helen, *Dark Wood and White Rose: Journey and Transformation in Dante's Divine Comedy*, Parabola Books, New York, 1989

McCormick, Elizabeth Wilde, *Surviving Breakdown*, Vermillion, London, 1997

MacDougal, Joyce, *Theatres of the Mind*, Free Association Books, London, 1986

Miller, Alice, *For Your Own Good*, Virago, London, 1987

Moore, Thomas, *Care of the Soul*, Harper Collins, London, 1992

—— *Dark Eros*, Spring Publications, 1994

Options Institute and Fellowship, 'Inward Bound', workshop programme at the Options Institute and Fellowship, Sheffield, Mass.

Perry, John Weir, *The Self in Psychotic Process*, Spring Publications, 1953

Rumi, *The Essential Rumi*, translated by Coleman Barks with John Moyne, Harper, San Francisco, 1995

Sachs, Oliver, *A Leg to Stand On*, Picador, London, 1984

Scheper-Hughes, Nancy, and Anne M Lowell, 'Psychiatry Inside Out: Selected Writings of Franco Basaglia', in Roy Porter (ed), *The Faber Book of Madness*, Faber, London, 1991

Schwartz-Salant, Nathan, *Narcissism and Character Transposition*, Inner City Books, Toronto, 1982

Shorr, Harriet, *The Artist's Eye: A Perpetual Way of Painting*, Watson-Guptill Publications, New York, 1940

Simpson, Joe, *Touching the Void* Pan, 1996

Sogal Rinpoche, *The Tibetan Book of Living and Dying*, Rider, London, 1992

Further Reading

The Spiral Path: Essays and Interviews on Women's Spirituality, Yes International, St Paul, Minnesota, 1988

Storr, Anthony, *Solitude*, Flamingo, London, 1989

Styron, William, *Darkness Visible*, Picador, London, 1992

Thich Nhat Hanh, *Peace Is Every Step*, Rider, London, 1991

Von Franz, Marie Louise, *Puer Aeternus*, Sigo Press, Santa Monica, 1981

Walsh, Roger, and Frances Vaughan (eds), *Paths Beyond Ego*, Jeremy Tarcher, Santa Monica, 1993

Wilde, Kate, 'Comparisons with hunter–gatherer societies of the American continent - environmental ethic and the shamanic role', BA dissertation, 1990

Wilhelm, Richard (trs), *I Ching: The Book of Changes*, Routlege, London, 1951

Young, Dudley, *Origins of the Sacred: The Ecstasies of Love and War*, Abacus, London, 1991

Index